Conquer
Email
Overload

Conquer Email Overload

WITH **Better Habits, Etiquette,** AND **OUTLOOK®**
TIPS AND TRICKS

PEGGY DUNCAN

P R E S S

ATLANTA, GEORGIA

Conquer Email Overload

Library of Congress Control Number: 2004094364

Book created entirely in Microsoft® Word. Screen captures made with Paint Shop Pro by Jasc Software, Inc.

Author photo by Philip McCollum Photography, Atlanta, GA.

Trademarks

To Maurice Threatt, my protector.

ACKNOWLEDGMENTS

I have to honor my mother, Verta Haskins, who taught me so many wonderful things; and my little brother, Bud, who always had to put up with me. And then came my son, who has always been more mature than I; and then his son, Christopher, who has given us all a reason to do better. And to three special people who kept me going throughout this process, Dr. Antonio Travis, Barbara Faison, and Traci Thomas, I thank you and appreciate you.

CONTACTING THE AUTHOR

Peggy Duncan provides training and consulting services that help individuals (or groups) save as much as eight weeks a year in wasted time, labor, and energy.

Requests for information about her services, as well as inquiries about her availability for seminars or computer classes, should be directed to the address below. If you have a comment or idea for this book, you are also encouraged to contact her:

Peggy Duncan c/o PSC Press, 1010 Pine Tree Trail, Atlanta, GA 30349-4979. You may also call 770-991-1316, or send an email to peggy@duncanresource.com.

Visit www.peggyduncan.com
for timesaving tips
and the free Webzine, **COPE**.
It's packed with tips to help you get
Clear-Organized-Productive-Efficient.

CONTENTS

Introduction

Billions of email messages cruise the Internet every day. This book is designed to help you stay in control with tips on how to format, compose, send, and manage the onslaught of this powerful communication tool.

Peggy Duncan has sat side-by-side with busy people just like you, teaching them how to better manage their email. This book is packed with tips from those sessions, as well as from the most frequently asked questions from her seminars.

We're going to explore Microsoft Outlook, the most robust email software on the planet, and discover solutions that are built to save you time. If you follow the step-by-step suggestions outlined in this book and set up your Inbox, you'll be able to move from one message to the next, finish quickly, and free up more time for important work.

Who Is This Book For?

Business professionals who are absolutely drowning in email will appreciate this book. It's written for people who already have Outlook installed, and are using it to process email. If you need help setting up Outlook, refer to the software's Help Menu and search on **accounts**.

Whether you've been using Outlook for years or are just starting out, you're going to learn tips and tricks in this book that you had no idea existed.

How Content is Arranged

This book approaches email management in three phases.

1. **Unload Your Inbox** - First, you must redefine how you use your Inbox; establish a routine for checking messages; and respond to requests in a timely manner. To help you find answers fast, you'll have to organize your paper and computer files. To help you follow up and follow through on the work, you'll learn tips in Outlook that will turbo-charge your Inbox and help you remember.

2. **Improve Your Image** - Second, you'll learn how important it is to treat email the way you would any other formal communication tool such as a letter. While it is important to have good writing skills, help with grammar, sentence structure, punctuation, and spelling is not what this book is about.

3. **Stay Out of Trouble** - Third, you'll discover how to avoid the trouble email can get you into by establishing a company email policy.

Managing the Inbox

To manage your Inbox, you have to stop using it for long-term file storage. It is for temporary storage, and every message that comes into it should be dealt with as it's opened.

The Inbox is **not** a:

- To do list for unfinished work.

- Calendar with meeting notices and reminders.

- Database for addresses, etc.

- Filing system for unfinished projects.

You're going to stop opening a message, looking at it, and closing it to review later. You're going to establish a routine for checking email and stick to it. This change in your work habits will be easier because you're going to follow the suggestions in the logical sequence that's laid out in this book. You must take time in this process to:

- Organize everything so you can find answers the instant you need them.

- Set up your Inbox with special toolbar buttons to help you act in an instant.

- Organize your folders for easy storage and retrieval.

- Use powerful, little-known features in Outlook that will speed up your work.

Improving Your Image

Learning powerful tips and tricks in Outlook is part of email management, but you should also take time to work on your email image with good format, composition, and distribution. You are judged on how you look, sound, and write. What message are you sending?

Staying Out of Trouble

Email is the most powerful communication tool in existence, and because any message can spread worldwide in a matter of minutes, you'll need to make sure you use it correctly to stay out of trouble. To do this, you must realize that email is not private, and with company-wide access, you have to ensure you take the necessary steps to monitor its use.

The time is now, and I understand that it seems impossible to control. But the more you put it off, the worse it gets. So go ahead and dress comfortably, clear the calendar, and close the door. Let's get this thing done!

Email does not have to be a burden.

GET ORGANIZED
AND FIND IT FAST!

If you want to be able to find what you're looking for the instant you need it, you'll need to get organized. When you're doing email, the faster you can find the answers, the faster you'll finish. If that makes sense to you, read on!

Principles of Organization

The principles of organization can be applied to any project or situation, whether it's organizing your garage or an office.

PRINCIPLES OF ORGANIZATION

- Purge on a regular basis, and keep only things you value or need.
- Give everything a home, and keep it there when you're not using it.
- Put everything near its point of use, and make it convenient to get to it, even if you have to buy two.
- Keep like items together.
- Use the right product to store it.

Once you know how to get organized, and you make a commitment to do it, it won't take you long to get it done. But I must prepare you: the real commitment comes in maintenance—it's something you'll have to do every day.

Getting organized might take you as little as six hours, but not getting organized can cost you as much as 240 hours a year!

How Much Is Your Time Worth?

Getting Started

Unfortunately, most people will make the decision to get organized after they've experienced some pain caused by the chaos. They may have lost a major client or possession, had serious health problems brought on by stress, had issues at home because they were never there, and so on.

Whatever the reason, it's past time you get started. So, stand in the middle of that mess you've created and close your eyes. Imagine how it could look. Imagine yourself living an organized life, instead of always scurrying around putting out fires. I know it's hard to imagine anything with all those piles, so let's create some order. Then you'll be able to think more clearly and can formulate a plan about what to do next.

With trash bags as your closest ally, choose which area you'll start with first. This will depend on what's important to you. If you have a small meeting table in your office that you really wish you could use, clear it first. If you feel embarrassed when people pass your office and see a bookshelf that's flowing over, start there.

On the one hand, this is a great place to start because the farther away you start from where you work, the more junk you'll find to throw out. But on the other hand, you might wear yourself out and get overwhelmed before you get to where the real work is done. I'll let you choose.

Knowing What to Keep and What to Trash

To end clutter (desk, computer, and Inbox), you'll have to make very brutal decisions about every file or piece of paper in those piles on the desk, on the floor, in the cabinets, and every other place you found to pack something. You'll have to decide what to keep and what to throw out or delete.

Should You Keep It? Ask Yourself:

- Have I referred to it in the past year?

- Can I get the information somewhere else?

- Do I need to keep it for legal reasons or is this something I value?

- If I throw it out and need it later, can I live with the consequences of having thrown it out?

Creating a Filing System That Works

To keep paper clutter from coming back, you'll need to set up a paper management system that is easy to maintain. A filing system should be logical so there is never any doubt about where you have filed something. Also, anyone else needing something in your files should be able to find it.

Here's how to create a logical filing system:

1. Only file things you really need to keep or value. Remember, at least 80 percent of the documents that come across your desk will probably never be referred to again. Why file it? And please don't send it to storage if it's junk.

2. Break down your job duties or business functions as if in an outline. Use the broadest categories first, then break them down. Use nouns, and keep like subjects together.

Marketing is a major portion of my business and a broad category. A partial example of how I subcategorized my Marketing files follows.

PARTIAL FILE INDEX

Marketing (Main category for this group. The plastic tab on this hanging folder should be in a distinctive color so you'll know at a glance when a new category starts.)

Advertising
Database
Future Ideas
Networking (organizations, networking groups I participate in)
    Club Pocket PC
    National Speakers Association
    SCORE Atlanta
Products
    Audio
    Books
    Catalog
Other
Public Relations
Campaigns
      Junky Office Contest
Media Kit
Seminars
Web Site
    COPE Webzine

Use interior folders inside hanging folders for easy access. If more than one interior folder goes into one hanging folder, stagger the tabs for easy viewing. To save time creating your filing system, check my Web site for my COPE WorkPak. It's a set of templates I use to get people organized. A complete File Index is included with the labels already typed.

This partial breakdown of files is all related to Marketing for my consulting business. I always know where everything is as opposed to looking in several different places for related material. A subject-based filing system like this will also help you when it's time to archive files (because you'll already have media types together–Accounting records not mixed in with Legal, etc.). Use the A-Z system only when it's a vendor- or client-only file, or something similar.

1. Create a filing index for all the files you'll keep. This way, you'll know approximately how many file folders to buy. The index is a complete breakdown of all the files you'll need to create. Put your index in the front of the file drawer (do this especially if others have to access your files, and if they're reference files).

2. Use hanging and interior file folders to help keep everything separated. Use a unique colored tab to distinguish the main categories. Use colorful folders that will reflect your tastes and lifestyle. If you belong to a sorority or fraternity, you might want to use those colors. If yellow and green make you feel alive, then create your filing system using those colors.

3. Type your labels or use a label maker. If you make your system neat and attractive, you'll take more pride in it, and will maintain it better.

4. If you can, arrange your hanging folders so they face you when you open the drawer.

5. Put all your plastic tabs in a straight line, one behind the other. This is a lot easier on the eyes than going from one end of the file drawer to the next to find a folder. (I prefer to put the plastic tabs in the front of the folder instead of the back.)

6. Test your system to see if others can find what they need.

7. Purge at least once a year.

While a document is in your hand, file it—don't pile it! Taking two seconds to put a document back into the file will save you minutes, and sometimes hours, the next time you look for it.

Organizing Your Computer Files

If someone sent you an email asking for a document you know is on your computer, how long would it take you to find it? A couple of seconds, minutes, hours, days, never?

As part of this process of managing email, it is just as important to organize your computer files as it is your paper files. The quicker you can find the answer, the quicker you will finish doing email.

Don't spend another day wasting time looking for something on your computer. With a good filing structure, using your same categories as you did earlier with paper, finding a document your boss just asked for will not be a problem. You will no longer procrastinate about getting back to someone because you can't find a file!

Using the same concept for establishing a paper filing system explained earlier in this chapter, you should create the same type of breakdown for your computer files.

Take time now to create your new computer filing system with the new folder structure; then move all files into their respective folders.

PURGE!

Creating New Folders in My Documents

This is how the computer filing system will be created.

1. Right-click the **Start** button, click **Explore**.

2. Scroll to find the **My Documents** folder, and double-click it to open.

3. Click **File**, point to **New**, then click **Folder**.

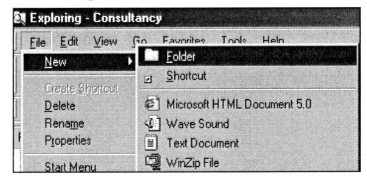

Figure 1. Create New Folders as you break down broader categories, keeping like subjects together.

4. Type the name "Business" for the new folder (on the right-side of the window), and press **Enter**.

   The new folder becomes a subfolder of My Documents.

Creating Subfolders

To create a subfolder, *you have to make sure you have the right folder open.* The open folder is indicated on the Address line. To create a subfolder of the Business folder, double-click it to open it first, then create the subfolder.

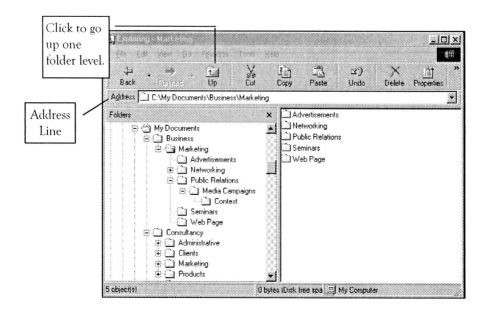

Figure 2. Shows a computer filing system breakdown that will make it easy to find what you need, especially when you're in a hurry.

Naming and Renaming Files

When you name your files, take advantage of the fact that you can use up to 255 characters. Name your files so you'll know exactly what the document is about without opening it.

To rename a file:

1. Right-click **Start**, click **Explore**, right-click the filename, and click **Rename**. The filename will become highlighted, and a black box will surround it.

2. Type your new filename, and click **Enter** or click anywhere off the name *twice* to deselect it.

Moving Computer Files to New Folders

If you have dumped all your files into the My Documents folder, or if you have a lot of folders but you skipped the broad categories mentioned earlier, you'll have to move all the files into the newly created folders.

1. Continuing inside Explore, double-click the **My Documents** folder so all the files you have created are on the right-hand side of the window.

2. On the left-hand side of the window, find your main folder (My Documents) and click (one click) all the plus signs next to all of its subfolders so all folders and subfolders belonging to My Documents are in view on the left-hand side.

3. Click a file on the right, and drag it to the appropriate folder on the left side of the window. The highlighted folder is the one in which the file will relocate to.

   ▪ If there are adjacent files you need to move to the same folder, click on the first file, and while holding down the **Shift** key, click on the last file in the group. All the files in the group will become selected.

   ▪ If you see files in nonadjacent locations you need to move to the same folder, click each file while holding down the **Ctrl** key. Each file will become selected.

   ▪ If you need to deselect a file, continue holding down the **Ctrl** key, and click on the file again.

Finding Files on Your Computer

1. Right-click the **Start** button, and click **Find** (or **Search**).

2. If you want to look for all files containing certain text, type the text in the **Containing text** box (or **All or part of the file name** box).

3. If you know the name of the folder or file, type it in the Named text box (if available), click the **Look in** drop-down arrow (or click the **Browse** button) to instruct

Windows where to look for the file, click **Find Now** (or **Search**).

4. If what you're looking for pops up before the system has finished looking, click **Stop**, then double-click the folder or file to open.

☛ *To narrow the search, complete other search criteria as indicated in the version of Windows you're using.*

Organizing Outlook

Improving email management not only involves organizing your paper files and computer files, but also your Inbox, Contacts, and your Calendar. The faster you find the answers, the faster you can get through email.

Organizing Your Inbox

To organize your Inbox, you'll use the same method described earlier for your paper files and computer files, starting with broad categories, and breaking them down. We'll go into more detail on this later in the book.

Organizing Your Contacts

Having instant access to your Contacts as opposed to having piles of business cards stuffed everywhere will help speed up your response time. You'll be able to find an important phone number and mailing or email address the instant you need it.

Organizing Your Calendar

Having the calendar part of Outlook makes it easy to drag meeting notices, to do's, reminders, and other information right from the Inbox to the Calendar.

UNLOAD YOUR INBOX

New messages coming in are not your problem, but rather the mess that's already there!

Yes, you get a lot of email messages every day. We all do. That's not the problem. The problem is that mess that's already in your Inbox that you haven't dealt with. You have hundreds or thousands of months-old messages that represent unfinished work, demands on your time, missed deadlines, and broken promises. You know they're there; they frustrate you every time you see the count, but you go day in and day out letting them pile up, with no end in sight.

For the most part, you can't control how many messages people send you. But you can manage what happens to them once they hit your Inbox. And letting them stack up unattended is not the answer. Ignoring them won't make them go away. You can get email under control, but you have some work to do before it can happen.

If email OverLOAD
is a problem,
DUMP the LOAD!

Establish a Routine

You should get into the habit of checking email at a certain time every day, maybe once in the morning and once in the afternoon. You should consider turning off the message notification box that comes up every time a new message comes in (click **Tools, Options, Email Options,** untick the box notification) so you won't get tempted to check all day.

Just as you do with paper, touch the message, and do something with it: either delete it, answer it, schedule it, forward it, file it, or flag it (or print it) for follow-up, or delegate it. To help you decide which messages to keep, refer back to the questions you should ask yourself on page 7.

Set a deadline to be finished checking your email at each sitting. If you establish a deadline, say 30 minutes, and use the tips I'll outline here, you'll figure out a way to make it happen.

Use your Inbox
for temporary storage!

Turbo-Charge Your Inbox

Microsoft Outlook is the most powerful email client in existence. If you're busy, it's the one to use. But if you don't take the time to set it up right, all that power goes to waste. We're going to spend some time moving, changing, and adding items to your Inbox and some of the other folders associated with it. These small changes will revolutionize how you approach and deal with email.

> This may look like a
> lot of work, but it's not. And you'll
> only have to do it one time!

What Do You See?

To ensure we're all looking at Outlook the same way, please open it, and go to your Inbox. You should see the Folder List in the left pane. It contains Archive Folders and Personal Folders with your Calendar, Contacts, Deleted Items, Drafts, Inbox, Journal, Outbox, and Sent Items. To display the Folder List, click **View**, **Folder List**.

In addition to the Folder List, you may also want to see the Outlook Shortcut Bar (you won't necessarily need to see both). If you don't see it, click **View**, **Outlook Bar**. When dragging items from one place to the next, say from your Inbox to the Calendar, you can drag and drop either to a folder in the Folder List or to an icon on the Outlook Bar. If you right-click the Outlook Bar, you can add more items to it. Click through it to experiment.

Now check to ensure you have both the Standard and Formatting toolbars displayed. Right-click anywhere on a toolbar, and click **Standard**. Repeat and click **Formatting**.

Finally, if Word is your email editor, please turn this feature off. Click **Tools**, **Options**, **Mail Format** *tab*, untick the box, **Use Microsoft Word to edit email messages**.

At-A-Glance

The following is a quick view of the steps you'll need to take prior to going through the messages in your Inbox. The goal is to use some of Microsoft Outlook's best features, in ways you haven't thought of, to make managing email easier.

An explanation and step-by-step instructions for each of these techniques follow this section.

☞ *Reminder: Instructions are for the full version of Outlook, not Outlook Express. Most instructions work for Outlook 98 and up, except as noted.*

At-A-Glance – 40 Steps to Take

Pre-Work: Turbo-Charge Your Outlook Inbox	Done
STOP If you have not followed instructions up to this point and organized your paper and computer files, go back now! You don't want disorganization to slow you down (you won't be able to find answers fast). Take time to do this. You'll get all that time back and so much more! If you've gotten organized and are ready to move forward, let's do it. *As you move through these steps, always make sure you're inside the right window as indicated.*	☐
1. Investigate your Internet provider's privacy policy and make sure you're using one that won't sell your address to third parties. A free service is not worth the time you'll spend battling SPAM. Change providers if you need to.	☐
2. If you're busy and email overload is a problem, you should use the full version of Outlook. If you're not, stop now and get it. Come back to this book after it's loaded and ready to go.	☐
3. Develop a company-wide code to introduce subject lines in your email messages so the recipient knows at a glance what's expected (e.g., CALL; MEET; FYI; ACTION; BTW (by the way), etc.	☐

Pre-Work: Turbo-Charge Your Outlook Inbox	Done
4. Invest in a SPAM blocker if your company doesn't have one, and load it on your computer. See page 26 for the solution I recommend).	☐
5. **From the Inbox,** turn on the Junk Email feature (Adult Content also).	☐
6. **From the Inbox,** create a Rule that sends mail Suspected as Junk to the Deleted Items folder. RUN the rule now when prompted.	☐
7. Customize the **Inbox Toolbar** and add the *Send to Junk Senders List* button.	☐
8. Organize your **Inbox** using the same concept explained earlier for your paper and computer files. Create a folder breakdown, starting with broad categories, and keeping like subjects together. Spend sufficient time on this up-front.	☐
9. Add a **CYA** folder to your **Inbox** for all messages you'd rather keep because you need the evidence (if you don't know what CYA stands for, ask a buddy). Don't worry about creating a folder breakdown for this folder because you'll probably never need anything in it. If you do, you can always use the Search function to find it.	☐
10. **From the Inbox,** sort Date column with oldest at the top. (The oldest messages will be the majority of the ones you can delete.) ☞ *Once you clear your Inbox, you should re-sort your messages with the latest ones at the top.*	☐
11. Change the **Inbox** View to AutoPreview (if you have your virus software updated).	☐

Pre-Work: Turbo-Charge Your Outlook Inbox	Done
12. Adjust **Inbox** columns so you can see enough of the subject and the Received date.	☐
13. **From the Inbox**, create a Rule that colors messages that come from a significant sender (your boss, a major customer, etc.).	☐
14. **From the Inbox**, create a Rule that sends the boss's (or someone else's) mail to a certain folder. RUN the rule now when prompted.	☐
15. **From the Inbox**, create a Rule that sends messages with a certain subject line to a special folder.	☐
16. **From the Inbox**, create a Rule that delays each message you send by 2 minutes (or your time choice).	☐
17. Customize the **Inbox Toolbar,** and add the *Tasks* button.	☐
18. Customize the **Inbox Toolbar**, and add the *Task Request* button.	☐
19. Customize the **Inbox Toolbar**, and add a *Meeting Request* button.	☐
20. Open a **New Message**, and change the View to add the *Bcc* textbox.	☐
21. Customize the **New Message Toolbar,** and add a *Close All Items* button, and rename the button to display as "Close."	☐
22. Customize the **New Message Toolbar,** and add a *SEND* USING button (if you need it).	☐

Pre-Work: Turbo-Charge Your Outlook Inbox	Done
23. Customize the **New Message Toolbar**, and add a *MOVE TO FOLDER* button (if it's not already there).	☐
24. Open any message and customize any **Open Message Toolbar** to add a *Close* button.	☐
25. Open any message and customize any **Open Message Toolbar** to add the *Delete* button.	☐
26. Open any message and customize any **Open Message Toolbar** to add the *Task Request* button.	☐
27. Open any message and customize any **Open Message Toolbar** to add the *Meeting Request* button.	☐
28. Click the Task Request button to open the **Task Request Dialog Box**, and customize the toolbar to add a *CLOSE* button and a *Delete* button (as described above).	☐
29. **From the Inbox**, create a new message. Put no recipient, no subject line, etc. In the body of the message, type your Contact information. Close the message without sending it. It should automatically go into your Drafts folder to use later.	☐
30. **From the Inbox**, create a toolbar button that upon clicking it, a new email message will open addressed to a group of people you send the same message to with a subject line already filled in.	☐
31. **From the Inbox**, create a Signature with your contact information.	☐

Pre-Work: Turbo-Charge Your Outlook Inbox	Done
32. **From the Inbox**, create a script for information you have to send often as in directions to your office. Add these scripts as Signatures and give them recognizable names.	☐
33. **From the Inbox**, change your Options to switch your default email format to Plain Text.	☐
34. **From the Inbox**, change your Options to format your message text to wrap at 75 characters per line.	☐
35. **From the Inbox**, change your Options to Return to Inbox "After moving or deleting an item."	☐
36. **From the Inbox**, change your Options to **not** empty your Deleted Items folder every time you exit Outlook.	☐
37. Categorize your **Contacts** so you can filter them later.	☐
38. **Open Word** and customize its **Standard Toolbar**, and add the *Send Doc as Attachment* button.	☐
39. Turn off the feature that capitalizes the first letter of sentences (if this drives you crazy).	☐
40. Step through the other timesaving tips and tricks so you can maximize even more of Outlook's power.	☐

You can't control how many messages
people send you. But you **can** control
what happens to them once they
land in your Inbox.

STEP 1 Investigate your Internet provider's privacy
policy and make sure you're using one that won't sell your
address to third parties. A free service is not worth the time
you'll spend battling SPAM. Change providers if you need
to.

The Right Provider and Software

Having access to email is not a luxury—it's a necessity in today's
business world. Buying the best service, and paying a little extra
money to use it, is well worth it. If you're using a service that forces
you to visit its Web site to check your email, you're going to get hit
with a lot of distractions such as pop-up ads (press **Ctrl+W** to close
them or invest in a pop-up blocker), special deals, and links to sites
that have nothing to do with what you need or want to do.

If you think you're saving money by using a free email service,
you're mistaken. You're spending your money in the time you're
wasting battling all the junk that's getting through. And a lot of
these services sell your information to third parties, so you'll get hit
with even more junk.

Everyone reading this book won't have Outlook. If you want to
manage email efficiently, you need this feature-rich software. It has
built-in features that will help you be more productive by helping
you reduce junk email, and creating rules that specify what you
want done to certain messages as they arrive in your Inbox.

Check with ISPs that service your area for one that supports this software. If they support it, they'll be able to help you set it up. If they inform you that they only support Outlook Express, get the information anyway because it's usually the same for the full version of Outlook.

STEP 2
If you're busy and email overload is a problem, you should use the full version of Outlook. If you're not, stop now and get it. Come back to this book after it's loaded and ready to go.

Outlook: The Right Choice

The instructions outlined herein are for the full version of Microsoft Outlook 98-2002 (not Outlook Express). Instructions have not been thoroughly tested for Outlook 2003, but I've peeked at it, and it's very similar. I've noted some differences throughout the book.

STEP 3
Develop a company-wide code to introduce email subject lines so the recipient knows at a glance what's expected (e.g., CALL; MEET; FYI; ACTION; and so on).

Codes for Subject Lines

Whether you work in a traditional corporate environment or not, you could develop codes that spell out the purpose of your email.

EXAMPLE

Subject: CALL: Ms. Johnson would like you to call her tomorrow morning.

CODE	DESCRIPTION
CALL	The recipient is going to have to call someone.
MEET	Another dreaded meeting notice.
ACTION	The recipient has work to do.
FYI	For Your Information. No action needed. Message is for information purposes only.

*I use this same type of coding when scheduling appointments, preceding the calendar item with words such as EVENT, CALL, MEET, SPEAK. You can also color-code each appointment in version 2002 and above. Right-click on an appointment, choose **Label**, then **category**. You can also edit pre-defined Labels or set Automatic Formatting to do this automatically. (Anytime I create a CALL appointment, it automatically turns yellow.) To review this feature, right-click anywhere on a calendar page, and click Automatic Formatting. See Outlook's Help for details.*

STEP 4 Invest in a SPAM blocker, and load it onto your computer (or check with your IT department for solutions).

SPAM Blockers

It is estimated that SPAM comprises as much as 75 percent of online messages. And according to the Federal Trade Commission, about two-thirds of it involves some type of fraud. At this writing, SPAM legislation will do nothing to curb SPAM, but there is software on the market that will block it.

SPAM software is available as a stand-alone product that filters mail before reaching your email client (Outlook) or as an add-on that integrates with it. There are lots of options out there from free to annual subscriptions.

Do your homework or check with your IT department. Below is a partial list of SPAM sites and software.

Websites
www.SPAMhelp.org
www.zdnet.com (read reviews on different software)

Software – www.cloudmark.com has a wonderful, SPAM-fighting product called SpamNet that, in my opinion, is the absolute best. It's the only product I personally recommend. Everything else I tried was no better than Outlook's built-in capabilities. The software is subscription-based, and represents a community of thousands of people adding to a SPAMmers list.

Do Not Respond to SPAMmers

When you receive unsolicited email that is clearly junk, don't respond. Responding only verifies to the sender that you're a valid email address. Instead, add them to your Junk Senders list if your software has one, and delete the message without opening it. The Junk Senders list will block any future email coming from that sender.

Professional SPAMmers are smart. They're spoofing email addresses, making it harder to stop them. The product I mentioned above, SpamNet, is the best defense against unsolicited messages.

Join the Cause

You can help fight SPAM by visiting www.CAUCE.org, the Coalition Against Unsolicited Commercial Email, an ad hoc, all volunteer organization, created by Netizens to advocate for a legislative solution to the problem of UCE (a/k/a "SPAM"). Also visit www.junkemail.org for more help.

STEP 5 From the Inbox, turn on the Junk Email
feature (Adult Content also).

Junk Email Filter

If you're using the full version of Outlook 98 or above, you'll be able to use its powerful Organize feature to block junk email, or to automatically route messages from certain people or about certain topics to folders that you designate. (If you're using Outlook 97, a download for this feature is available on the Microsoft Web site.)

Outlook's junk email feature searches for commonly used phrases in your incoming messages. It can then automatically move a message from your Inbox to any other folder you specify (or change the color so it's easy to recognize).

To activate the junk email feature in Outlook 98 or above.

1. Click **Tools, Organize**.

2. Click **Junk email** (you won't see this feature if you haven't set Outlook up to handle your email).

3. Click the **turn on** button for **Junk** and **Adult Content** to activate the feature.

Add to the Junk Senders List

The junk email filter is a great feature, but it's a long ways from being sufficient in blocking SPAM. Some junk will still make it through. When it does, it's easy to add a sender to the Junk Senders list.

1. From within the Inbox, right-click on the unopened message, point to **Junk Email**.

2. Click **Add to Junk Senders list**.

Oops! Delete Someone from the Junk Senders List

At some point, you might add someone to your Junk Senders list by mistake.

1. From within the Inbox, click **Tools**, **Organize**, **Junk Email**.

2. At the bottom of the resulting dialog box, click to see more options (see light gray text).

3. Click **Edit Junk Senders**.

4. Once inside the Junk Senders list, type the first letter of the email address you're looking for, and scroll until you find the correct one.

5. Select it, and click **Delete**.

Add an Established Junk Senders List to Your Computer

I'd spent a lot of time adding email addresses to my Junk Senders list on my desktop computer. When I bought my laptop, I didn't want to have to start from scratch, so I added the desktop list to the laptop list.

On the computer with the Junk Senders list you want to copy.

1. Click **Start**, point to **Find**, then click **Files or Folders**.

2. In the **Named box**, type **Junk Senders.txt**.

3. Click **Browse**, and double-click on **C:,** then on **Application Data**. (If you don't have this folder breakdown, skip this step and go to Step 4.)

4. Click **Find Now**.

5. When the file is found, double-click it to open it.

6. Click **File**, **Save As**, and save the file onto a diskette by placing a: in front of the file name. Leave the file name the same.

When you get to the new computer, follow the same steps, but replace the file that's on the new computer with the file you saved on the diskette.

Use Your Signature to Discourage Junk

A lot of people absolutely do not enjoy receiving jokes, thoughts for the day, chain letters, and all those other email messages so many of you feel compelled to send. They want you to stop, but they're too embarrassed to ask.

Create an automatic signature (see instructions on page 62) that will go out with every email you send that says something similar to: "Please do not add my name to your distribution list for jokes, prayers, thoughts for the day, chain letters, etc. Thanks!"

Ask People You Know to Stop Sending You Junk

Develop a spiel to send to people you know who are sending you junk that goes something like this:

"I appreciate your thinking about me, but in an effort to streamline my email messages and manage my time, I have to ask you to remove my name from the distribution list you're using. Thanks!"

If this doesn't work, call them and ask them to stop. Be firm.

STEP 6 From the Inbox, use the Rules Wizard to
create a Rule that sends mail Suspected as Junk to the
Deleted Items folder.

Rules Wizard

Now that you've turned on the junk email feature, you can create a
rule that says anything from any address on your Junk Senders list
or any item that is suspected of being junk email (or that contains
adult content) is to be automatically deleted (or moved, colored,
etc.) from your Inbox.

1. From within the Inbox, click **Tools**, **Rules Wizard** (or
   display the Advanced Toolbar by right-clicking anywhere
   on a toolbar and clicking **Advanced**. Click the **Rules
   Wizard** *toolbar button*), then click **New**.

2. Select **Check messages when they arrive**, and click **Next**.

3. Scroll to find the condition, **suspected to be junk email or
   from Junk Senders List**, and tick the box next to it and next
   to **Adult content**. Then click **Next**.

4. Tick the box next to **delete it**; then click **Next**.

5. Look at the Exceptions list, and tick if any of them apply to
   your situation; then click **Next**.

6. Tick the box next to **Run Now** to run the rule on messages
   presently in your Inbox (this helps when you have lots of
   old messages you never bothered to delete).

7. Make sure the **Turn on the rule** box is ticked, and click
   Finish.

STEP 7 Customize the **Inbox Toolbar** and add the

Send to Junk Senders List button.

Customize Your Toolbar

You can customize any toolbar and put the Add to Junk Senders list toolbar button on it. (Depending on your version of Outlook, the instructions may vary, but they'll be similar enough to follow.)

1. From inside your Inbox, right-click on any toolbar button. Then click **Customize** (or you can click **Tools, Customize**).

2. Click the **Commands** *tab*. On the Categories side (on left), click **Actions** (because that's what you would click on the Menu bar to get to this feature).

3. Now on the Commands side (on right), scroll down to find **Add to Junk Senders** list (not Junk Email).

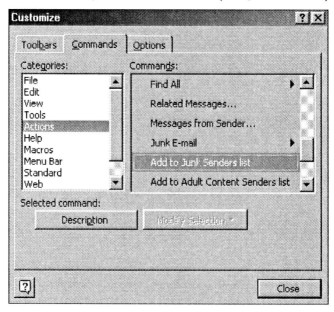

Figure 3. Customize your toolbar, and set it up to fit the way you work.

4. Once you find **Add to Junk Senders list**, click on it, and drag it up to the toolbar, and drop it (put it where it suits you).

    As you drag, the **I**-beam indicates where the toolbar button will go when the mouse is released. Leave the Customize dialog box open for now. Once you have placed your new toolbar button, you can rename it or change it to an image.

5. With the dialog box still open, right-click on your new toolbar button (or click Modify Selection).

6. Click inside the **Name** box, and type the name you want (make it something short like JUNK so the button will be small).

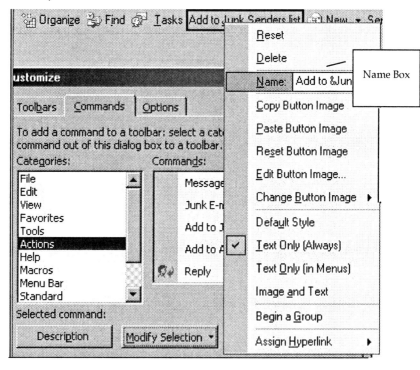

Figure 4. Drag your Add to Junk Senders List button to quickly add email addresses to this list. Rename the button once it's placed on your toolbar.

7. **Or**, you can change the button image by pointing to **Change Button Image**, and clicking an image, then **Close**.

- If your toolbar button has words and an image on it and you only want an image, with the Customize dialog box still open, right-click the toolbar button again, and click **Default Style**. **Close** when you're finished.

8. While in the Customize dialog box, you can remove a toolbar button by clicking on the button, and dragging it down off the toolbar (you'll probably have to do this to make room for your new button. Remove the buttons you don't use, but find out what they do first.)

- If you're not in the Customize dialog box, and you want to remove a toolbar button, hold down the **Alt** key, and drag the button off the toolbar.

Now that you've customized your toolbar and added the Junk button to it, you won't have to add to your Junk Senders list one message at a time (the following feature may not work in Outlook 2003).

9. From inside your Inbox, hold down the **Ctrl** key, and select each message that's junk.

10. Click the **Junk Senders** button that you added to your toolbar. All the junk messages will be added to the Junk Senders list one by one.

11. Then, while all the junk messages are still selected, click **Delete** (or press the **Delete** key on your keyboard).

☞ *To bypass the Deleted Items folder, hold down the **Shift** key as you click **Delete**.*

STEP 8 Organize your Inbox using the same concept you used for your paper and computer files. Create a folder breakdown, starting with broad categories, and keeping like subjects together. Spend sufficient time on this up-front.

To get started organizing your Inbox, you'll need the Folder list in view. If you don't see it, click **View**, **Folder List**.

Organize Your Inbox

To make retrieval of messages easier, and to keep your Inbox free of old messages, you can create subject folders to subcategorize your Inbox.

Purge first, then create your folders. You should use the same concept for creating an Inbox filing system using broad categories as you learned for your paper files on page 7.

Separate Messages Into Folders

1. Create all your main folders first. From within the Inbox, click **File**, point to **New**, click **Folder**.

2. Name the new folder.

   If you put a number in front of the folder name, you can have them appear in a particular order. For instance, if you keep messages coming from your clients, create a main Inbox folder called "1Clients." Then, create subfolders for each client (or put all messages in the Clients folder if you won't have many).

   If you have messages you need to follow up on later, either create a "2FollowUp" folder in your Inbox (or desk), flag the message for follow up, or drag the message to your computer calendar icon or folder to set a reminder (Close the message before you attempt to drag it. Outlook 2003 will automatically move a message to a follow up folder when you flag it).

Another option, and perhaps the best one, is to **move the message** (instead of dragging) to the calendar, and set up a reminder date. If you move the message to the calendar without dragging it, the message will be contained inside an envelope. Later, if you need to resend the message as a follow-up, you won't have to locate it. To move a message from the Inbox, either click the **Move to Folder** toolbar button , or right-click the message, and click **Move to Folder** (or **Ctrl+Shift+V**). Later, if you need to open the message envelope, double-click it.

Putting the number "1" in front of Clients will make that folder appear first in your Inbox folder list. Putting the "2" in front of FollowUp will make it appear second in your folder list, and so on.

3. To select where you want the new folder to be, click once on **Inbox**, and click **OK**.

4. Repeat until all your main folders have been created.

5. Create subfolders of the main folders by repeating the steps, but instead of selecting Inbox as you did in Step 3, you'll select the appropriate main folder.

6. Click and drag the messages already in your Inbox that you need to put into the new folders. (Use the same method of moving email messages into the folders that you used when moving computer files on page 12.)

Purging vs. Archiving

In Outlook, you can Archive old files automatically after a certain number of days.

- In Outlook 2000, click **Tools**, **Options**. Then click **Other** *tab*, **AutoArchive**, and make your selections.

- In Outlook 2002, click **Tools**, **Mailbox Cleanup**, and make your selections there.

But why send junk to storage?

While it's true this is a quick way to "clean up" your Inbox, that's not the solution you need. You have to get out of the habit of filling up your computer with useless junk. (Confession: I AutoArchive my Sent Items folder automatically every three months. To set this up, right-click on your **Sent Items** folder, click **Properties**, **AutoArchive** *tab*, tick desired settings. I only archive this folder because if it's in my Sent folder, that means it required some action on my part, so I want to keep it.)

Deal with your email as it hits your Inbox. This is the ultimate solution that will keep you stress- and worry-free about important work that may be falling through the cracks, customer requests going unanswered, or potential business that's going unnoticed.

STEP 9 Add a **CYA** folder to your Inbox for all

messages you think you need to keep as a backup (if you don't know what CYA stands for, ask a buddy). Don't worry about creating subcategories for this folder because you'll probably never need anything in it. If you do, you can always use the Search feature to find it.

Create CYA Folder

If you're in a corporate environment, you probably like to keep a lot of old emails to CYA. Try creating a folder called CYA (or something nicer), and drag all these types of messages into it (don't worry about separating these messages into other folders since you'll probably never need them).

You'll probably never need any of it, but I know it'll make you feel better having it. If you ever need to find anything in the folder, use the Find feature explained below to locate it. Purge every three months.

Find Email Messages Fast

You won't need to use this feature in your Inbox after this process (because it'll be clear), but you may need to find a message in your Sent Items folder.

Several features will help you find an email message quickly. You can:

1. Sort messages by field (From, Subject, Date Received, etc.) by clicking the appropriate field heading. For example, if you want to sort the messages by subject, click the **Subject** heading. To reverse the order, click Subject again.

Figure 5. From inside your Inbox, you can click on the column headings, and sort your messages quickly.

Outlook's **Find** feature is another way to locate email messages fast. You can type any portion of a From name, subject, or any text in the message in the **Find** dialog box.

1. Click **Tools, Find** (or click the **Find** toolbar button).

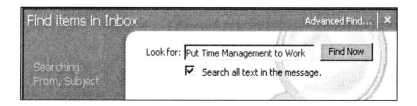

Figure 6. Use the Find feature, and type any portion of a From name, subject, or any text in the message.

2. Enter your text in the **Look for** text box, click the **Search all text** box; then click the **Find Now** button (or press **Enter**).

3. Click **Clear Search** to restore your Inbox to its original state. (Click **Advanced Find** if you need more options on finding messages that meet certain conditions.)

☞*Another way to find all messages from a particular sender or with the same subject line is by opening one of the messages, clicking* ***Actions, Find All, Related Messages*** *or Messages from Sender.* ***Or*** *you can view messages with the same subject lines by clicking* ***View, Current View, By Conversation Topic.***

STEP 10 Sort Received Date column with oldest at

the top. (The oldest messages will be the majority of the ones you can delete.) (Once you clear your Inbox, re-sort your messages with the latest ones at the top.)

Sort Received Date Column

Click to Sort

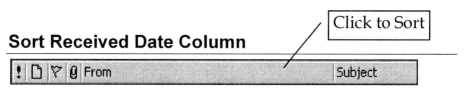

Figure 7. Clicking on From will sort your list by Sender. Clicking on Subject will sort list alphabetically by Subject, and so on.

Clicking on any column heading will sort the items in your Inbox. Click it one way, and it'll sort ascending. Click again, and it'll sort descending (or vice versa depending on how you have it sorted).

When you're going through the process of clearing messages that have piled up, sort so your oldest messages are at the top. These will be the majority of the ones you'll delete without following up, etc. Once you finish clearing your Inbox, re-sort to put the newest messages back on top.

STEP 11 Change how you view your Inbox.

Change How You View Your Inbox

Views give you different ways to look at the same information in a folder by arranging and formatting it differently. Two views give you a glimpse of parts of messages before you open them.

1. Click **View**, **AutoPreview** or **Preview Pane**. (Viewing messages like this could activate certain viruses because the message is opened. Keep your anti-virus software updated if you use either of these views.)

With AutoPreview, you will see a few lines of the message without opening it. With Preview Pane, the entire message will open in a window below your messages. From within the Preview Pane, you can open attachments, follow a hyperlink, respond to meeting requests, and display properties of an email address.

Other views include Unread Messages, Last Seven Days, By Conversation Topic, and more. Click **View**, **Current View**. Then click each one to experiment with the result.

You can set a different view for each Inbox folder, which comes in really handy. I set my follow-up folder to AutoPreview, and my New Messages Inbox to Messages. If I don't recognize the sender or if the subject line makes no sense, I usually delete unopened.

☞ *If you display your Advanced Toolbar, you will have access to a drop-down box to quickly choose the view you want. To display this toolbar, right-click anywhere on a toolbar, and click **Advanced**. The drop-down box is labeled **Messages**.*

STEP 12 Adjust Inbox columns so you can see enough of the subject and the receipt date.

Adjust Inbox Columns

Figure 8. You'll want to adjust the Subject column to view more of it because SPAMmers add text at the end of legitimate-sounding subject lines.

1. Hold your mouse over the right border of the column you want to adjust.

2. When your mouse becomes a double-headed arrow, drag the column to the desired width.

STEP 13 From the Inbox, create a rule that colors messages that come from a significant sender (your boss, a major customer, and so on.).

Color Messages from Certain Senders

You can create a rule to have messages from certain senders automatically change color.

1. From inside the Inbox, click once on a message from anyone for which you'd like to set up this rule.

2. Click **Tools, Organize**, select the **Using Colors** option, and choose desired color.

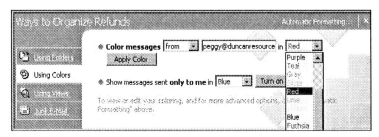

Figure 9. This instruction tells Outlook to color any message coming from me Red as it enters your Inbox.

STEP 14 From the Inbox, create a rule that sends the boss's (or someone else's) mail to a certain folder. Run the rule now when prompted.

Send Message from Certain Sender to Special Folder

Earlier in this section, you were instructed to organize your Inbox folder into some logical sequence (page 35). Now you can create rules that automatically send messages from certain domains or from certain people into a particular folder (you can also create a rule that takes a message coming in from a particular person and sends it to someone else).

1. From inside the Inbox, click once on a message from anyone you'd like to set up this rule for.

2. Click **Tools**, **Organize**. The **Using Folders** option should be highlighted.

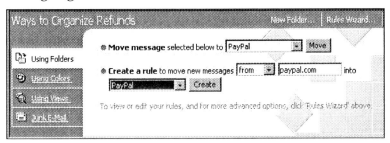

Figure 10. I created a rule that sends any messages coming to me from Paypal.com to a folder I've named PayPal. When the instruction is simple, this is the feature to use. However, for more complicated rules, you should use the Rules Wizard.

3. The Create a rule portion of Organize should already have the email address you selected. If not, complete the dialog box as desired.

4. Select the folder to which you want messages from this person to go. When you click the drop-down box, if you don't see the folder you want, click **Other folder**, select the desired folder, click **OK**.

5. Click **Create**, and click to **run the rule now** on messages already in your Inbox.

In the future, messages coming into your Inbox from this address will automatically go to this folder.

☞ *If you set this up, you may want to change an email option that will keep any replies you send to these messages inside your same folder. This will keep the thread together. Click **Tools**, **Options**, **Email Options**, **Advanced**. Tick the option, **In folders other than the Inbox, save replies with original message**.*

STEP 15 From the Inbox, create a rule that sends

messages with a certain subject line to a special folder. (You'll have to use the Rules Wizard to create this Rule because it's not coming from the same sender, page 31.)

Move Messages With Certain Subject Line

You might not need this rule right away. Here's how I use it. Every month, I send an email message letting subscribers of my free Webzine, COPE, know that the new issue is on my site. Included in the notice is the option to Unsubscribe. Here is the Unsubscribe text from my message:

> **To unsubscribe, click this link:**
> **mailto:drgroup@duncanresource.com?subject=Unsubscribe COPE.**

On the rare occasion that someone unsubscribes to COPE, and clicks the Unsubscribe option in my message, their message comes into my Inbox with UnsubscribeCOPE in the subject line. Outlook recognizes the rule I created that automatically sends this message into the Unsubscribe folder, and sends it there. For more information on using the Rules Wizard, refer to page 31.

STEP 16 From the Inbox, create a rule that delays

each message you send by two minutes (or your time choice up to two hours).

Delay Delivery of All Messages

Have you ever sent a message, and the instant you clicked Send, you wanted to get it back? One way to get it back is to retrieve the message (if you're on a Microsoft Exchange Server). But this could end up being a big mess if you sent to a group of people. You might be able to retrieve some, but not all, depending on whether the recipient has already opened it or not.

Another solution is to **Delay Send** (this is what I did). You could create a rule that instructs Outlook to hold your messages in the Outbox for a certain length of time before it sends them. But you'll have to remember that if you want to send a message and log off immediately, your message will still be in your Outbox (Outlook will warn you).

To set up Outlook to delay delivery of all messages, follow these steps.

1. On the **Tools** menu, click **Rules Wizard**, then click **New**.

2. Click **Start from a blank rule** (you won't see this choice in Outlook 2000, but keep going).

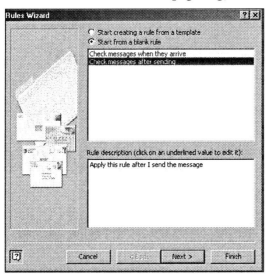

Figure 11. To create a rule that delays sending your messages, you'll start with a blank rule.

3. Tick **Check messages after sending**, then click **Next**.

4. Click **Next** to have this rule apply to all messages, or, to limit the messages that the rule applies to, in the **Which condition(s) do you want to check** list, select any options you want before clicking **Next**.

5. In the **What do you want to do with the message** list, select **defer delivery by a number of minutes** (delivery can be delayed up to two hours).

6. In the **Rule Description** box, click the underlined phrase, **a number of**, and enter the number of minutes you want messages held before sending.

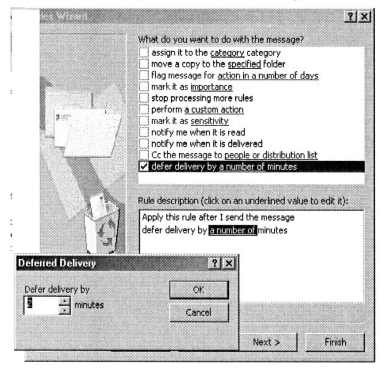

Figure 12. Always read the dialog box text. It guides you throughout the Wizard to set up your rules. Here, I've decided to defer delivery by two minutes from the time I click Send.

7. Click **OK**, then click **Next**.

8. Select any exceptions, then click **Next**.

46

9. In the **Please specify a name for this rule** box, type a name for the rule.

10. Click **Finish**.

Delay Delivery of a Single Message

You may want to create a message but not have it delivered until later. Here is how you can set this up for a single message.

1. In the message, click **Options** [🔲 Options...] .

2. Under **Delivery options**, tick **Do not deliver before**.

3. Enter the delivery date and time you want.

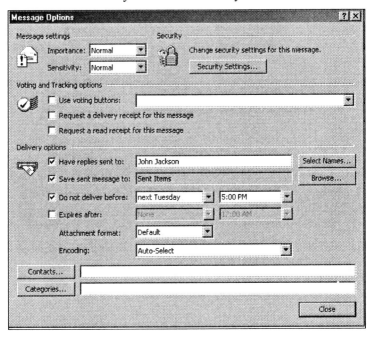

Figure 13. If you choose not to delay delivery of all messages (page 44), you can opt to delay delivery of a single message (you can't do both). Notice here that I'm also having the replies to this message sent to someone else. John Jackson is one of my Contacts, so Outlook will automatically plug in his email address. Also in this box, minimize your use of Delivery and Read receipts (they add to more email clutter).

STEP 17 Customize the **Inbox Toolbar,** and add the *Tasks* button.

Add Tasks Toolbar Button

You should add the Task button to your Inbox toolbar to make it easy to check all tasks that you've added (either for yourself to complete or work that you've delegated).

To add the Tasks button, follow the same steps to customize your toolbar as outlined on page 32. The Tasks button under is under View. Refer to Outlook Help for more information on using Tasks.

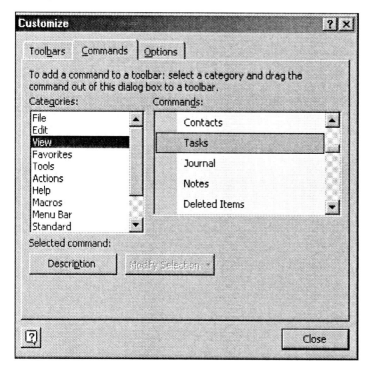

Figure 14. Move your Tasks toolbar button up to join your other toolbars. In this instance, you should be in the Inbox view.

STEP 18 Customize the **Inbox Toolbar**, and add

the *Task Request* button. ⬚ *(Step 17 adds the Task button. This is the Task Request button.)*

Add Task Request Toolbar Button

You should add the Task Request button to your Inbox toolbar, and use it when you're delegating work or asking a favor of a friend. I'm suggesting you add it to your Inbox toolbar because the task goes out like a regular email message.

When you click the Task Request button, a New Email Message window opens. You'll type in your recipient, subject, and information as you would a regular email message.

If you have an email message that's associated with the task, insert it as a Text Only Item (click Insert, Item, find message, tick Text Only). When you click Send, the message will go out as an email, and the Task will be automatically added to your Tasks list. (To add the Task Request button, follow the same steps to customize your toolbar as before (page 32). The Task Request button is under the File Category.)

STEP 19 Customize the **Inbox Toolbar**, and add a

Meeting Request button.

Add Meeting Request Toolbar Button

Get off the phone! Instead of making endless phone calls trying to set up meetings, use the Meeting Request function. If you're using Microsoft Exchange at your company, and everyone uses Outlook's calendar, you can check schedules for free/busy times, send a request, and wait to see if it's accepted or rejected.

☛*If you use Outlook 2002 or higher, Microsoft has a service that will allow users to share schedule information no matter where you are. You join the service and use a shared location on the Internet for publishing your free/busy times. For more information, visit the Microsoft Office Internet Free/Busy Service at http://freebusy.office.Microsoft.com/freebusy/freebusy.dll.*

To add the Meeting Request toolbar button, you'll use the same steps for customizing your toolbar as before (page 32). To create a meeting using Meeting Request, you can either start by using the Meeting Request button, the Menu bar, or by creating the meeting on your calendar first.

1. Click your new **Meeting Request** toolbar button (or from the Calendar view, click **Actions**, **New Meeting Request** (or click **Ctrl+Shift+Q**). Or you can create the meeting on your calendar as you normally would.

2. If you're using Microsoft Exchange, you could then click **Scheduling** (Outlook 2002 or higher) or **Attendee Availability** (in earlier versions), and view other people's calendars (based on the permission levels they have set).

   If you're not using Microsoft Exchange or the Free/Busy service mentioned earlier, send the meeting request as a regular email (it works the same way).

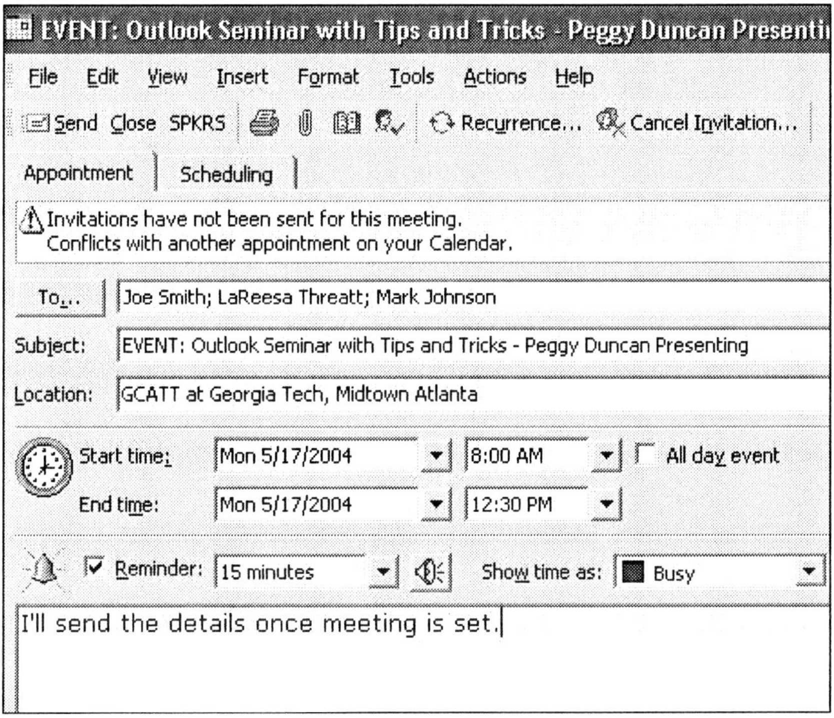

Figure 15. Setting up a meeting using Meeting Request will keep you off the phone. The request goes out as an email message, and the recipient will Accept or Reject or send alternate date/time. After people start accepting or rejecting, a Tracking tab will appear in the Meeting dialog box to help you keep track of responses.

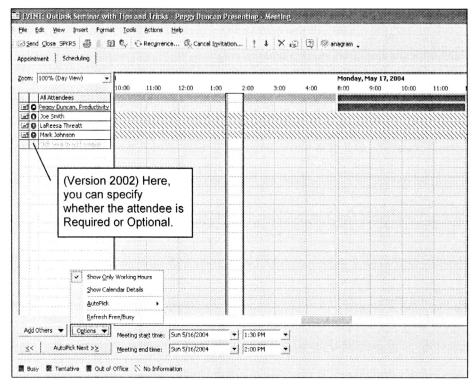

Figure 16. With Microsoft Exchange, on the Scheduling tab, you can Add Attendees, view their availability, and have Outlook AutoPick a time and date everyone is available.

STEP 20 Open a **New Message,** and add the Bcc
option.

Add Bcc to Protect Recipients' Privacy

Use the Bcc option when you're sending messages to several people and you want to keep the recipient list private.

1. Create a new message.

2. Click **View, Bcc Field**.

To use this feature later, you'll create a new message as you normally would, address the message to yourself, and add the recipient addresses on the Bcc line.

STEP 21 Customize the **New Message Toolbar,**
and add a *Close All Items* button, and rename the button to read "Close."

Add Close All Items Toolbar Button

If you add a Close button to the New Message Toolbar, it makes it less confusing to close a message (the X close confuses me because I'm not sure if I'm closing the window I'm currently in or if I'm closing the program).

From your Inbox, you'll follow the same steps as before to customize a toolbar and add a new button to it (page 32). The Close All command is located under the File Category. To save space on the toolbar, rename the button to read "Close."

STEP 22 Customize the **New Message Toolbar,**
and add a *SEND USING* button (Outlook 2000. You won't need to do this in later versions).

Add Send Using Toolbar Button

If you create more than one email account, you may decide to use different ones to send a message, depending on what you're sending (e.g., a different one for personal and business. I use the same email account regardless of what I'm sending because I don't want to have to remember to change.

If you add the *Send Using* button to a toolbar, it'll make it more convenient to choose the account you want to use for a message. With Outlook 2002 or above, you can click the **Accounts** button inside a new message to do this.

From your Inbox, you'll follow the same steps you've followed throughout this process to add a new toolbar button (page 32). The Send Using command is located under the File Category (Outlook 2000).

STEP 23 Customize the **New Message Toolbar**, and add a *Move to Folder* button (if it's not already there).

Add Move to Folder Toolbar Button (Ctrl+Shift+V)

You'll want to use the Move to Folder command when you're inside a message and need to file it in one of your folders. I use this feature most often when I need to move a message from the Inbox to my Calendar for follow up. When I move the message, it's placed as a Calendar item inside a message envelope. So later, when I need to follow up on the message, I double-click the envelope, and it's right there.

From inside a New Message, you'll follow the same steps as before to add a new toolbar button (page 32). The Move to Folder command is located under the File Category. The shortcut to move a message to a new folder is **Ctrl+Shift+V**.

STEP 24 Open any message and customize any

Open Message Toolbar to add a *Close* button.

Add a Second Close All Items Toolbar Button

Adding the Close All button in this view makes it convenient to close whatever you're working on. From any Open Message, you'll follow the same steps as before to add a new toolbar button (page 32). The Close All command is located under the File Category inside your Customize Toolbar dialog box.

STEP 25 Open any message and customize any

Open Message Toolbar to add the *Delete* ⊠ button.

Add a Delete Toolbar Button

Adding the Delete button in this view makes it convenient to delete whatever you're working on. From your Inbox, you'll follow the same steps as before to add a new toolbar button (page 32). The Delete command is located under the File Category.

STEP 26 Open any message and customize any

Open Message Toolbar to add the *Task Request* button.

Add a Task Request Toolbar Button

You should put the Task Request toolbar button in this view because a lot of times you'll read a message that will require you to delegate a request or ask for a favor. Having the Task Request button displayed in this view simplifies this.

Sending a request using the Task Request feature automatically adds it to your Tasks list. You'll also be able to set a due date. The person on the other end Accepts the task, and it is automatically added to their Tasks list as well.

From any Open Message, you'll follow the same steps as before to add a new toolbar button (page 32). The Task Request command is located under the File Category.

STEP 27 Open any message and customize any

Open Message Toolbar to add the *Meeting Request* button.

Add a Meeting Request Toolbar Button

You should put the Meeting Request toolbar button in this view because a lot of times you'll read a message that will require you to set up a meeting. Having the Meeting Request button displayed in this view simplifies this.

From any Open Message, you'll follow the same steps as before to add a new toolbar button (page 32). The Meeting Request command is located under the File Category.

STEP 28 Click the Task Request button to open the

Task Request dialog box, and customize the toolbar to add a *CLOSE* button and a *Delete* button.

Add Close and Delete Buttons to Task Request

Sending a request using the Task Request feature automatically adds the task to your Tasks list. It also gives you the opportunity to set a due date. The person on the other end Accepts the task, and it is automatically added to their Tasks list as well.

Before you send a Task Request, you should include your contact information. And sometimes you may want to add a file to the request. By default, Outlook does not add your signature to Task Requests. I've added a workaround to this shortcoming on page 57, but for now, add the Close **Close**, and Delete ✗ buttons inside the Task Request dialog box.

STEP 29 Create a dummy New Message with your contact information in it.

Create a Signature for Task Requests or Meeting Requests

You'll need the information in this message when you send a Task Request or a Meeting Request. A shortcoming of these Request features is that when you send the request to someone, your automatic Signature (you'll create later) doesn't accompany the message (more information on Signatures can be found on page 62).

As a workaround, you'll create a dummy message with all your contact information in it and save it into your Drafts folder (messages you create and save, but not send, automatically go into your Drafts folder).

1. Create a New Message. Put no recipient, and type My Signature in the subject line.

2. In the body of the message, type all your Contact information in a format similar to addressing a letter.

3. Close the message without sending it. It should automatically go into your Drafts folder to use later.

Add a Signature to a Task Request (or Meeting Request)

Now that you've created a draft message with your Contact information in the steps above, you're ready to add a Signature to a Task Request or Meeting Request.

1. Click to send a Task Request and complete the body of the message as you normally would.

2. To add the Signature workaround you created above, click **Insert** on the Menu.

3. Choose to insert an **Item**.

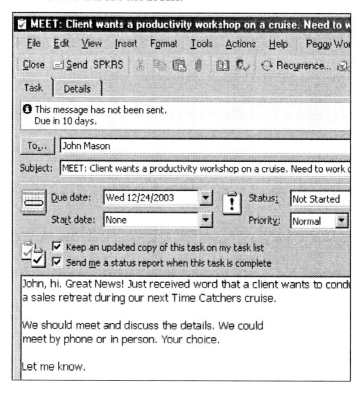

Figure 17. Here, you're sending a task request as a task email. As a professional courtesy, you'll need to Insert your Signature as an Item so the recipient will have your contact information.

4. Click your **Drafts** folder once to display its contents.

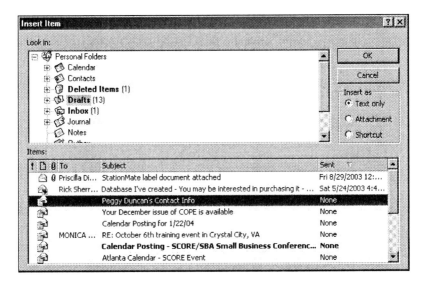

Figure 18. By default, Outlook doesn't add your Signature to the Meeting or Task Request (and you can't get to it). The workaround is to create a script with your contact information, save it in the Drafts folder, and insert it as a Text Only Item anytime you need it.

5. Tick the Insert as **Text Only** option.

6. Double-click the file with your contact information.

7. Click to **Send** your message as you normally would.

STEP 30 From the Inbox, create a toolbar button

that upon clicking it, a new email message will open addressed to a group of people you've already designated, and with the subject line already filled in.

Create a Toolbar Button to Send Messages

This is a great feature to use if you have a very select group of people you send special messages to. Here is how I created my toolbar I named "SPKRS". When clicked, a new message opens with my recipient names/email addresses and the subject line already filled in. You should feel comfortable doing this because you've already learned how to customize the toolbar (on page 32. You'll find the New Message toolbar under the File category).

1. Customize your Inbox toolbar, and add the **New Message** button to it.

2. Right-click on your new button.

3. Click inside the **Name box,** and type SPKRS or whatever you want to call your button.

4. Then click **Text Only (Always).** The drop-down menu will close.

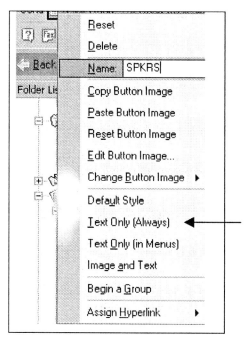

Figure 19. You can customize your toolbar button using words or graphics.

5. Right-click the button again.

6. Point to **Assign Hyperlink,** and click **Open**.

7. On the left side of the Assign Hyperlink dialog box, click **Email Address**.

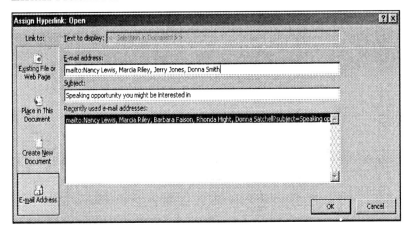

Figure 20. Email addresses in this hyperlink should be separated by commas.

8. Now on the right side of the dialog box, in the **Email address** textbox, type the names of the people you want added to the list, using a semi-colon to separate each name (the word mailto: will appear).

    ☞ *If you type names instead of email addresses, this will work as long as these people are in your Outlook Contacts with email addresses.*

9. If you want to always use the same subject line with this message, type it in the Subject textbox.

10. Click **OK** and **Close**.

☞ *Experiment with creating toolbar buttons and hyperlinking them to a certain Web page. You'd follow these same instructions, but instead of hyperlinking to an email address in Step 7, you would choose the **Existing File or Web Page** option. And in Step 1, you'll need the **Search the Web** button located under the Web Category. Similarly, you can also hyperlink to any file or application.*

Later, you may want to add or delete names to this group.

1. Right-click on any toolbar, and click **Customize**.

2. Then right-click on your button you want to change (my SPKRS button).

3. Point to **Edit Hyperlink**, click **Open**, and make your changes.

Create a Toolbar Button to Forward to Group Automatically

Sometimes I'll receive an email message about a speaking opportunity that I want to Forward to my special networking group (as described in Create a Toolbar Button to Send Messages on page 59). I repeated the steps and added this same SPKRS button inside the Forward view (putting the button here doesn't work in Outlook 2000).

1. Open any message, and click to **Forward** it as you normally would.

2. Then follow the same steps as described previously to add the button.

STEP 31 From the Inbox, create a Signature with enough detail about who you are and your contact info.

Create a Signature to Identify Who You Are

Avoid sending people messages without your contact information. You can set up your Inbox to automatically add this information to almost every message you send in what's called a Signature.

Your email signature is also a great place to let people know the types of messages you prefer not to receive. Here's how you can have this information, along with your address, phone number, etc., automatically print at the bottom of every email message you send in Outlook.

1. Click **Tools**, **Options**,

2. Click the **Mail Format** tab.

3. Click the **Signature Picker** (or **Signatures**) button at bottom, click **NEW,** name the signature, tick **Start with blank**, click **Next**.

4. Add all your contact information, spacing paragraphs and line breaks as you normally would.

5. Add a message that will limit the junk from people you know: "Please do not add my name to your distribution list for jokes, prayers, thoughts for the day, chain letters, etc. Thanks!"

6. Click **Finish, OK**.

7. Next, let Outlook know you want this signature to appear at the bottom of each message by clicking the **drop-down box** just above the Signature Picker (or Signatures) button. Choose the default signature you want, **OK**.

☞ Later, *if you want to change your Signature, follow steps 1-3, and click **Edit**. Then click **Advanced Edit, Yes** to view your Signature in WordPad or NotePad (it will be easier to format).*

Identify Yourself Using Email Account Preferences

Another way to help recipients know who you are (and another great way to self-promote) is to add information people will see on the From line when they receive a message from you.

1. From the Inbox, click **Tools**, **Accounts** (or **Email Accounts**).

2. Choose **View or change existing email accounts**, **Next**.

3. Double-click the account you want to change.

4. In the **Your Name** *box*, add desired information. Mine says "Peggy Duncan, Productivity Training, Consulting, Products.

5. Click **Next, Finish**. Change information for each account as needed.

STEP 32 Create a script for information you have
to send often as in directions to your office. Add these scripts as Signatures and give them recognizable filenames.

Create a Script as a Signature

You may have to send someone the same information often, as in directions to your office. You can create the information and save it as a Signature, and pop it into an email message anytime you need to.

You should follow the same instructions for creating a Signature as described earlier (page 62). But instead of adding your contact information, you'll type the directions to your office.

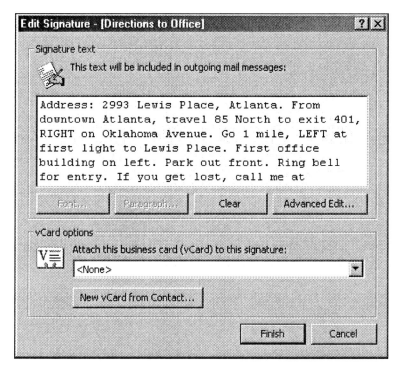

Figure 21. With information you send regularly, create it and send as a Signature.

After clicking **Finish,** you'll need to select your default signature so that it prints in your messages by default instead of directions to your office.

The next time you need to send someone directions to your office, you'll create your message as you normally would, click the Signature button that should be on your New Message dialog by default (or click **Insert, Signature**), and click "Directions to Office." (If you don't see the Signature toolbar button by default, customize the toolbar and put it there. You'll find it under the Insert Category. You'll use the same instructions to customize your toolbar as on page 32.)

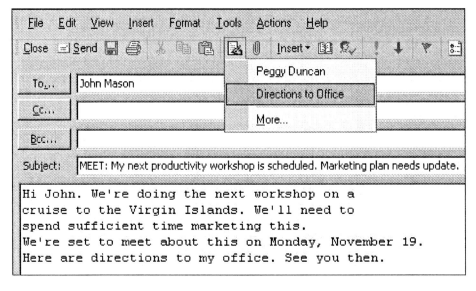

Figure 22. Having information you send regularly as a Signature is a big timesaver.

STEP 33 From the Inbox, change your Options to switch your default email format to Plain Text.

Use the Plain Text Message Format

Consider using the Plain Text format as some email clients may not recognize your fancy format, artwork, HTML, etc., or your recipient has turned this feature off.

To be on the safe side, make the Plain Text format your default, and use HTML only when you have to.

1. From inside the Inbox, click **Tools**, **Options**, **Mail Format** *tab*,

2. Choose **Plain Text** format.

☛ *I've realized that if you use the HTML format and send an attachment, if the recipient does not use Outlook, the attachment will drop*

*off. (Learn how to send an attachment from inside a message on page 83.
Learn how to send an attachment from Word on page 75.)*

STEP 34 From the Inbox, change your Options to

format your message text to wrap at 75 characters per line.

Wrap Text for Shorter Sentences

Shorter lines of text are easier to read. You can change your default
to automatically wrap text after a certain number of characters for
each line.

1. From the Inbox, click **Tools**, **Options**, **Mail Format** *tab*.

2. Click **Internet Settings** (or Settings).

3. Change as desired (the screen below is from Outlook
   2002. Outlook 2000 is slightly different).

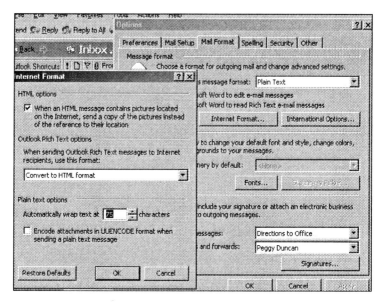

*Figure 23. Shorter lines of text are easier to read. You can change
your default to wrap text.*

Short Text Lines, Long URLs

If you're concerned about long Web links splitting up in your messages after you reduce the line length, there are several free services that make it easy to transform a long URL into a very short one. Visit the following sites: www.snipurl.com and www.tinyurl.com.

STEP 35 From the Inbox, change your Options to return to Inbox "After moving or deleting an item."

Change Options to Return to Inbox

When moving through email, as you finish one message, you'll want to return to the Inbox to decide what you'll do next, instead of having to deal with the message that automatically opens next.

1. From inside the Inbox, click **Tools**, **Options**, **Email Options**.

2. Click the drop-down box, and choose **return to the Inbox**.

STEP 36 From the Inbox, change your Options to **not** empty your Deleted Items folder every time you exit Outlook.

Do Not Empty Deleted Items Folder Upon Exit

By default, Outlook may be set up to automatically empty the Deleted Items folder every time you exit Outlook. Turn this feature off because your junk filter may have deleted a valid message and you want to have the chance to check.

1. From inside the Inbox, click **Tools**, **Options**, **Other** *tab*.

2. Untick the box next to **Empty the Deleted Items folder upon exiting**.

On another note, to keep this folder from piling up, as you delete items, holding down the **Shift** key as you click the **Delete** button (or press the Delete key) will permanently delete the item from your computer, bypassing the Deleted Items folder.

☛*To make this feature even more convenient, you may want to turn off the warning box that pops up every time you attempt to delete an item. If so, click **Tools**, **Options**, **Other** tab, **Advanced Options**, and untick the box next to **Warn before permanently deleting items**.*

STEP 37 Create Contacts and categorize them so you can filter them later.

A fine-tuned database will help you breeze through email. You'll be able to find any phone number or address you need the instant you need it. Your Outlook database is your Address Book. Within the Address Book, you'll have Contacts, Personal Address Book, or Global Address Book. I only use the Contacts folder. If you're on an Exchange network, you'll have access to a Global Address Book in which everyone in your company can share.

I've worked with a lot of people who literally spend hours looking for someone's phone number. They've been collecting business cards for years and just continued to add to the piles they already had. Taking the time now to either scan that stack of cards into your computer, or type new Contacts, or hire someone to do it will ultimately save you a lot of time.

Create Contacts – Your Outlook Database

Creating Contacts is easy in Outlook.

1. From the Contacts folder, click the **New Contact** toolbar button ⬛ or **Ctrl+N**.

2. Click inside each field (or tab to each field, or press Enter), and type the appropriate information. You do not have to click Full Name or Address. Clicking inside the field and typing is a better timesaver. (Refer to Outlook Help for more details if needed.)

3. Click the **Save and New** button ⬛ as you finish each to start another (add a Category for each Contact as described below). If you need to add another Contact from the same company, click **Actions, New Contact from Same Company**.

4. If you need to close a Contact without saving it, click **File**, **Close**, and don't save changes. To save and finish, click **Save and Close**.

➡️*If you want to change how your Contact name is displayed (First Name, Last Name or Last Name, First Name), click **Tools**, **Options**, on the **Preferences** tab, click **Contact Options**, and choose.*

Categorize Your Contacts

As you update your Contacts, one of the fields you may not have noticed is where you'd add a Category. Adding a Category to each person in your database makes it easy to filter a list later and send messages to people meeting certain criteria.

An example is my Clients category. If I need to send an email message only to them, or produce mailing labels for a special invitation or holiday card, I can filter my Contacts, pulling out just the people in my Clients category, and create customized email messages, mailing labels, etc., using mail merge (see instructions on creating a mail merge email beginning on page 85).

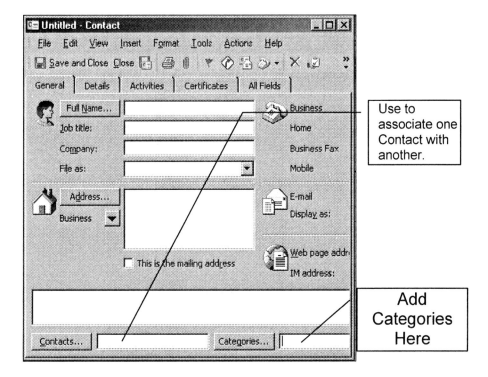

Figure 24. Adding a Category to each Contact makes it easier to filter them later, only mailing to people who fit specific criteria. To the left of the Categories button is Contacts. Click this button, or type the person's name, to associate one contact with another (e.g., an administrative assistant to the manager).

Add Categories to Each Contact

First, take a look at the Categories that come with Outlook by default. Delete the ones you don't need, and add ones you do. Think about all the organizations you belong to, people with similar jobs, and so on.

For new Contacts, add the Categories as you go, making sure you enter the exact category name. For example, you shouldn't establish a category titled "Clients", then type "Client" as the category. If you do, you'll end up with both.

1. Click the **New Contact** toolbar button.

2. At the right bottom, click the **Categories** button.

3. Scroll to see if your new categories are already listed as a Category.

4. If not, click the **Master Category List** button, and type your new category, being consistent with each entry.

5. Click **Add**, **OK**, **Cancel**.

If you already have lots of names in your database, you'll have to endure the arduous task of adding a Category to each one. But think about it like this: you'll only have to do this one time, and will know to do this up-front from now on.

To quickly add Categories to contacts you already have in your Outlook database:

1. From Contacts, click **View**, point to **Current View**, click **Phone List**.

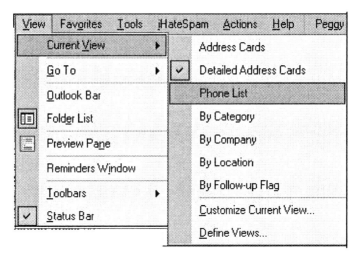

Figure 25. Displaying your Contacts by Phone List will make it easy to scroll down to each Contact and add a Category. You should develop your Category list first, and keep everything consistent.

2. Scroll to find the **Categories column** heading, and click, drag, then drop that column right next to the **Full Name column**.

If you don't see the Categories column, you'll have to add it (right-click anywhere on the toolbar next to Full Name, left-click **Field Chooser**. Click and drag the Categories button, to this same toolbar).

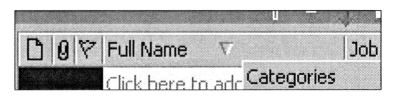

Figure 26. Once you display your Contacts, moving the Categories column right next to the Full Name column will eliminate your scrolling back and forth. If you don't do this, you'll soon see why you should. The red arrow indicates where the column will land once you release the mouse.

3. Now with Full Names and the Categories column right next to each other, you can easily go down the list and add the appropriate Category (to see the Category list in this view, right-click the Contact, and click **Categories**).

Later, if you want to change how you view your Contacts, repeat Step 1.

Filter Recipients by Categories

If you've already added Categories to your Contacts, you can quickly send an email to any Category (or you may want to create a Distribution List (or group). More information on distribution lists is on page 93).

1. From Outlook's Contacts view, click **View**, point to **Current View**, click **By Category**.

2. Click the desired **Category** once to select it.

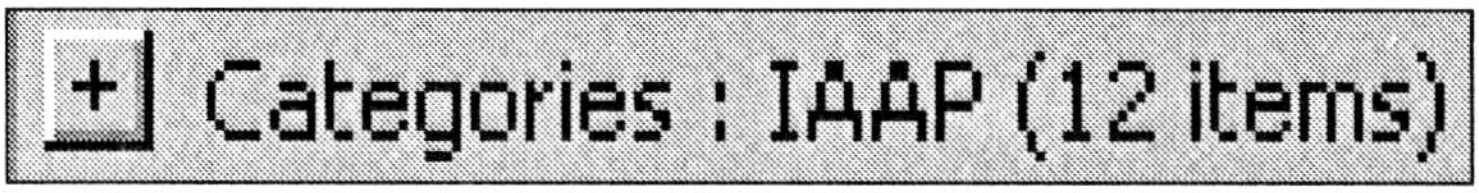

± Categories : IAAP (12 items)

Figure 27. Clicking the + sign will display all Contacts in this Category.

3. With the Category selected, click the **New Message button** (or click the Category and drag it to the Inbox folder). Your addresses will be on the To line.

4. Type your message, and click **Insert** to place your **Signature**.

5. Send the email as you normally would.

Bcc (blind copy)

You may not want all recipient names shown in the email. You can instead put addresses on the Bcc line (you turned on the Bcc feature on page 52).

1. Click on at least one of the email addresses now on the To line.

2. Press **Ctrl+A** to select all addresses; then drag all of them down to the Bcc line.

3. Type your email address on the To line (you're sending to yourself and blind copying others). Send the email as you normally would.

Find a Contact

Once you have your database set up, finding that important phone number will be easy. From inside your Contacts folder, in the textbox next to your Address Book toolbar button ▦ (located on the Standard toolbar), type any part of the name of the person you're trying to find, and press **Enter** (pressing **F11** will move the cursor to the **Find a Contact** box. If more than one choice is displayed, double-click the one you're looking for.

STEP 38 Open Word and customize its **Standard**
Toolbar, and add the *Send Doc as Attachment* button.

Customize the Word Standard Toolbar for Attachments

Adding the Send Doc as Attachment button to your Word toolbar will make it easy to send the document you're working on as an attachment in an email message. Once you add the button, you'll click it, and the Outlook New Message dialog box will open with your document already attached.

Open Word and customize your Standard toolbar as you have before (page 32). The Mail Recipient (as Attachment) Command is located under the File Category.

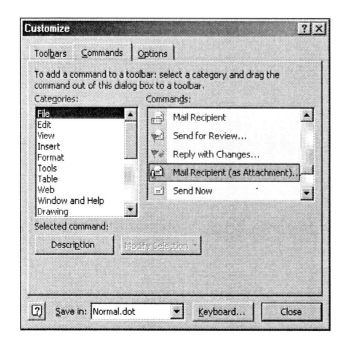

Figure 28. Adding this toolbar button inside Word will make it easy to send the document you're working on as an attachment in an email.

➤ *Your automatic Signature will not be at the bottom of a message you send like this. Before you send, click **Insert**, **Signature**, and choose the appropriate one for this message. If you're using Word as your email editor, you may not see Signature under Insert.*

STEP 39 Stop the automatic capitalization of the first letter of sentences if this drives you nuts.

Stop Automatic Capitalization of First Letter of Sentences

In Outlook 2002, you can turn off the feature that automatically capitalizes the first letter of sentences. This feature drives me crazy, so I thought I should let you know about it.

1. In Outlook 2002, click **Tools**, **Options**, **Spelling** *tab*.

2. Click **AutoCorrect Options**.

3. Untick the box next to "Capitalize first letter of sentences."

Spelling Check

You should notice in the same dialog box above that this is where you'll turn on Spelling Check if you want it.

Add Words to a Custom Dictionary

Once you turn on Spelling Check, you may want to add your industry or company jargon to the dictionary so your software will recognize them and not mark them as errors.

In the same dialog box as above, click to **Edit the Custom Dictionary** and add words to the list, pressing **Enter** after each.

STEP 40 Step through the following timesaving

tips and tricks to maximize even more of Outlook's power.

More Timesaving Inbox Tips

Messages People Send to You

Open Multiple Email Messages at Once

Once you clear the Inbox of the few messages that got past your SPAM filter, your Outlook Junk Filter, and your rules, you might glance through your Inbox and decide that some messages will need to be read before the others.

You can quickly open all these messages at once.

1. From the Inbox, press the **CTRL** key, and click on each message you want to open.

2. When you've finished selecting all of the messages, press **CTRL+O**, and each message will open, one behind the other.

Edit the Subject Line of Messages You Receive

You probably receive many messages with poor subject lines, some having absolutely nothing to do with the message (don't pull up an old message to someone and send them a new, unrelated message. Instead, create a fresh, new message).

You can edit the subject line of a message someone sends you.

1. Place your insertion point in the subject text and add or change what you need. (To select the entire subject line, triple-click it.)

2. Close the message, and click **Yes** to save your changes.

Edit a Message Someone Has Sent You

Sometimes before I file a message someone has sent me, I add a comment to it to help me remember a decision I made about it, the action I took, and so on.

To edit a message someone has sent you, from the open message:

1. Click **Edit, Edit Message** (or right-click the body of the message).

2. Click inside the message, then add your comments (I precede my edits with "Note from Peggy").

3. Then click the **Move to Folder** toolbar button (or **Ctrl+Shift+V**), and file as desired.

☞*As usual, if this is something you do often, customize your toolbar to add this button to it.*

Clean Up Emails and Get Rid of Carets (>>)

When you copy text from an email message, it may need some cleaning up before you can use it. For example, it may have lots of caret (>, ^) or unwanted paragraph marks at the end of each line that you'll need to get rid of.

Here are the steps you'd use. (If you rarely use text from emails, you'll think of many other ways to use the Find/Replace feature.)

1. **Copy** the text from an email message, **Paste** into Word.

We'll first get rid of all the >.

2. Press **Ctrl+H**.

3. In the **Find what box**, type > (or >> if you needed).

4. In the **Replace with box**, leave it blank (to replace > with nothing).

5. Click **Replace All**, then leave the Find and Replace dialog box open.

And/or you may have lots of ^.

6. Type ^ in the **Find what box** and **Replace All**, and leave the Find and Replace dialog box open.

You might also have to get rid of all the extra paragraph marks that may be at the end of each line. (These instructions will also remove the blank spaces you will now have at the beginning or end of each line in the text.)

7. Select only the text you want to change because all your paragraph marks will be removed.

8. Repeat the steps above, but type ^p in the **Find what box** and **Replace All**. (You're finding all paragraph marks and replacing them with nothing.)

9. Click **No** to checking the remainder of your document.

If you decide not to remove the extra paragraph marks, but need to remove the blank spaces at the beginning and/or end of each line in the text (that occurred when you removed all the >).

10. Select the text you pasted (or press **Ctrl+A** to select the entire document).

11. Press **Ctrl+E** to center the selected text, then press **Ctrl+L** to re-left-align it. All extra spaces will be gone.

Add People to Contacts from Inside a Message

You can add people who send you emails to your Contacts. I do not recommend turning on the feature that does this automatically. Do you really need everyone you send an email to in your database? You'd end up with a lot of email addresses in it, and will have no idea who the people are or why you kept the information in the first place.

But sometimes you will want to add them. Here's how.

1. Right-click on their name or email address on the From line.

2. Click **Add to Contacts**. A Contacts dialog box will open with their name and email address already filled in.

3. Complete information as appropriate, remembering to assign a Category (see page 70).

☞ *If all you see is a person's name on the From line, and you want to see what their email address is, double-click the name to display Properties.*

Look Up Contacts While Reading Their Message

You can quickly look up someone's contact information from inside a message they've sent you (if they're listed in your Contacts). From inside the message, right-click the information on the From line, and click **Look up Contact**.

Use anagram™ for Contacts / Calendar Appointments

A great timesaver for adding people to your Contacts is anagram™ (**www.getanagram.com**) software from Textual. If someone's contact information is in the body of an email message, inside a document, or on a Web page, all I do is select the text and click a button. In a flash, anagram adds the information to a New Contact dialog box, putting it all in the right places.

The same thing happens when I select information that resembles meeting information: anagram moves the information to my calendar. This is an incredible product that has saved me a lot of time.

➡ *If you have a lot of business cards stacked up everywhere, consider buying a business card scanner, scan the cards, then throw them out.*

Open or Save Multiple Attachments

Managing messages with multiple attachments will go faster if you open or save them all at once.

1. To open all messages at once, hold down the **Ctrl** key, and click on any of the attachments you want to open (or click one file, then press **Ctrl+A** to select all of them).

2. Click **File**, **Open**.

If you want to *save all the attachments*, that's even easier.

1. Without selecting any of the attachments, click **File**, **Save Attachments**, **OK**, and save in desired location.

Find Documents in Your Inbox With Attachments

If you ever need to search through messages that have attachments, use Outlook's feature to find all messages with attachments.

1. From the Inbox, click **Tools, Advanced Find**.

2. In the Look for box, choose **Messages**, click the **More Choices** *tab*, tick "Only items with," and choose "one or more attachments."

3. Click **Find Now**, and save results as desired.

Extract Attachments from Outlook Folders

The Outlook Attachment Sniffer lets you extract or remove attachments from all or selected Outlook folders. You choose where you want to put the files. For details, visit www. rsbr.de.

Determine What You've Already Done with a Message

Sometimes you can get so busy, you'll forget whether you've already replied to or forwarded a message. Icons next to your messages indicate what you've already done with them.

In your Inbox, you'll notice an open envelope icon next to the original (read) message.

- A small arrow overlapping the envelope icon, pointing to the left, indicates *you have replied to the message*.

- An arrow pointing to the right indicates *you forwarded the message to someone else*.

You can find out the date and time of your reply by opening the original message and reading the yellow Infobar (i) just above the From line (version 2002 and above). To see the details of your reply, choose "**Click here to find all related messages**." Advanced Find automatically launches and searches the default Inbox, Drafts, and Sent Items folders.

Messages You Send

Send an Attachment

It's easy to add an attachment to an email message. From inside your message, click the Insert File toolbar button [U]. Find the desired document, and double-click it to add to your message.

☞ *As soon as you type the word "attached" in your message, stop right then and attach the file so you won't forget.*

Send a Message to a Contact Quickly

Here are three quick ways to send a message to one of your Contacts (from the Contacts view).

- One way is to drag the Contact to the Inbox on your Outlook Bar or Folder List.

- Another way is to right-click the Contact, then click **New Message to Contact** on the shortcut menu.

- Or you can click once on the Contact, then click the **New Message** toolbar button.

☞ *If a person is in your Contacts and you're sending them a message, you don't have to click the To button to look up an email address. Instead, type the name in the **To** textbox, and Outlook will find it for you. If you have two people with the same name, Outlook will let you resolve (double-click the one you want).*

Prevent Addresses from Popping Up – AutoComplete

When you type a name or email address in the To, CC, or Bcc field of an email, Outlook displays a list of suggested email addresses (versions 2002 and above). You can delete all or some of these names from the cache so they don't appear (AutoComplete).

1. Use the arrow keys on your keyboard to select the bad address (or when the address you want to hide appears).

2. Press the **Delete** key to delete it (the address will remain in your Contacts, but won't be suggested to you by Outlook).

☞ *Or you can turn this feature off. From the Inbox view, click **Tools**, **Options**. On the **Preferences** tab, click **Email Options, Advanced Email Options**. Then, untick the "**Suggest names while completing To, Cc, Bcc fields**" box. (This feature has also been called AutoSuggest.)*

Retrieve a Message You Just Sent

If you're on a Microsoft Exchange server, and the recipient uses Outlook, you can recall a message before the person reads it. But as I mentioned earlier (page 44, Delay Delivery of All Messages), this could end up being a mess if you're not careful.

To recall a message after you've sent it:

1. Open your **Sent Items** folder.

2. Double-click the message you want to recall.

3. On the **Actions** menu, tick **Recall This Message**.

4. To recall the message, tick **Delete unread copies of this message**.

5. To replace the message with another one, tick **Delete unread copies and replace with a new message**.

6. Click **OK**, then type a new message.

7. Tick the **Tell me if recall succeeds or fails for each recipient** check box if you want to be notified about the success of your efforts. Good luck!

8. Click **OK**.

Resend a Message

If you need to resend a message that someone swears they didn't get (or to send the same message to someone else), it's easy to resend the message.

1. Find the message in your Sent Items folder and double-click it to open.

2. Click **Actions**, **Resend This Message**. Send it as you normally would.

3. If you need to resend the message, but to different recipients, delete the current list and enter the new names.

Have Replies to Your Messages Sent to Someone Else

In Outlook, if you're sending an email message and you want the replies to go to someone other than yourself (e.g., your virtual assistant), it's easy.

1. From within the New Message dialog box, click **View**, **Options**.

2. Click inside the textbox to the right of "**Have replies sent to**."

3. Either type the name or email address you want replies sent to, or click **Select Names**, find the address in your Address book, and double-click the name. Then click **OK** (only applies to current message).

Create Mail Merge Emails

Previously in this book, I discussed how you can add Categories to each of your Contacts so you can filter them and send information to specific groups that meet certain criteria (page 70). If you've done this, you could then send a mail merge email that addresses each recipient by name, just as you would in a mail merge letter.

(Or you can select the names in Contacts, and in Step 1 below, you would choose View, Only selected contacts.)

The instructions below assume you have added Categories to your Contacts.

1. From **Contacts**, click **View, Current View, Customize Current View**.

2. Click the **Filter** *tab,* then click the **More Choices** *tab.*

3. In the **Categories** *textbox,* either type the name of the Category you want to send an email to or click the **Categories** *button* to find it.

4. Click the **Advanced** *tab.*

5. In the **Field** *drop-down box,* point to **E-mail fields**, then click **E-mail**.

6. Next to the E-mail Field, under **Condition**, choose **is not empty**. (You have to do this because you're telling Outlook you only want Contacts in a certain Category who have email addresses listed in your database.)

7. Click **Add to List** to add **E-mail** to your filtering criteria.

8. Click **OK** until you're back to your Contacts. You will now only see Contacts who meet the criteria.

9. Now you're ready to do the mail merge. Click **Tools, Mail Merge**.

10. Choose **All contacts in current view**.

11. Under **document file**, choose either **New document** if you're creating something from scratch, or choose **Existing document** if your document already exists. We're going to do a new document.

12. Now under **Merge** options at the bottom of the dialog box, the **Document type** is **Form Letters**. Under **Merge**

to, choose **E-mail**. Then type a subject line for your email message. Click **OK**.

13. Your Contacts will export to Word, and Word will open. You will then create your mail merge document as you normally would, adding desired fields (if you do not know how to create a mail merge document, refer to Word's Help).

14. When finished creating your document, in Word 2002, click the **Merge to E-mail** toolbar button located on the Mail Merge toolbar (or you may want to see a sample of the document first by merging to a New Document, then email later). *In Word 2000 or below, you'll click the **Merge** button, then click **Merge**.*

15. Click **OK** to send your message to **All records** and in **HTML** format (has to be in HTML format).

More Timesavers

Email

Sync Other Email Accounts to Outlook

If you have miscellaneous accounts with various providers such as Hotmail, MSN, aol, etc., save time checking your messages by finding out how to sync all your email with Outlook (if possible). You'll then be able to check all messages at once, right from Outlook, without having to visit a company's Web site, get distracted by ads and entertainment news, and waste more time. Visit your program's Help section, and search on "sync" or "Using with Outlook."

Type International Characters with AutoCorrect

If you type international characters with accents, save time by using Outlook's AutoCorrect feature (version 2002 or above).

1. In most Microsoft software, to type a name with an accent, say María, you'll type Mar

2. Then hold down the **CTRL** key and type the apostrophe '.

3. Then **release the CTRL** key, and now type the **i**. The accented i will appear.

While this method is much quicker than inserting symbols, there is an even better way to do this. Using AutoCorrect (version 2002 and above), you'll instruct Outlook to replace a word typed one way with another way automatically.

1. Click **Tools**, **Options**, **Spelling** *tab*, tick the box **Use AutoCorrect when Word isn't the e-mail editor** (if blank), then click the **AutoCorrect Options** *button*.

2. In the **Replace box**, type Maria.

3. In the **With box**, type Mar, then hold down the **CTRL** key. Type the apostrophe ' then release the **CTRL** key.

4. Type **i**, then **a** to finish the name, and click **Add, OK**.

Now every time you type María, the accent will automatically appear. Other international characters include:

If you want à	CTRL+` (Accent Grave, left of the 1 key at top of the keyboard), the letter a, e, i, etc.
If you want â	CTRL+Shift+^ (Caret, #6 key at top of keyboard), the letter a, e etc.
If you want ã	CTRL+Shift+~ (Tilde, left of the 1 key at top of the keyboard), the letter a, e, i, etc.
If you want ä	CTRL+Shift+: (Colon), the letter a, e, i, etc.

Figure 29. If you type international characters often, but not enough to use the international settings, you may want to use the AutoCorrect feature.

☞ *If you use Outlook as your email editor, this feature only works with plain text and rich text format. If you use Word as your email editor, it works with all formats. I use Outlook as my editor because odd things have happened when I tried Word.*

Print Portion of a Message

Save printer ink by only printing the part of a message you need. If a message comes in formatted as HTML:

1. Select the part of the message you want to print.

2. Click **File**, **Print**, **Selection**, **OK**.

If the message is in plain text, you can edit the message, change the format to HTML, then print a portion of it.

1. Click **Edit**, **Edit Message**.

2. Click **Format**, **HTML**.

3. Repeat Steps 1 and 2 above.

Flag Messages for Follow-Up

You can flag a message for follow-up and assign a date and time to do the work (**Ctrl+Shift+G**). To use it, simply click once on the message (open or closed message), then click the **Flag** toolbar button. Click the **Due by** drop-down box and set the reminder date. (You can also open a Contact and flag it for follow-up.)

Before Outlook 2003, I never recommended using this feature because you had to leave the message in your Inbox in order for the reminder to appear (in Outlook 2003, any message you flag automatically goes into a Follow-Up folder, and the reminder appears right on schedule). If you're using Outlook 2002 or earlier, instead of flagging a message, consider dragging the message to your calendar and setting a calendar reminder. Or you can add the information to Tasks.

If you'd rather have each reminder pop up in its own box the way older versions of Outlook worked, consider a product called, **Talking Alarm Clock** by CinnamonSoftware.com. The only drawback to using this software is that it does not integrate with Outlook. But for critical reminders, I take advantage of its really great interface and features. And best of all, the software is a free download.

If you prefer to have software that integrates with Outlook, visit www.slovaktech.com, and review the **Reminder Manager**. For a small fee, this product provides reminders from any folder.

Use Keyboard Shortcuts

Following is a list of keyboard shortcuts you may prefer using. To view an entire list of keyboard shortcuts for Outlook, click **Help, Microsoft Outlook Help**. Click the **Index** *tab*. In the textbox, type the keyword, **shortcut**, and click **Search**. Then double-click the topic, keyboard shortcuts. Under "What would you like to do", click the desired link.

Message Keyboard Shortcuts	
Check for New Mail	F5 or Ctrl+M
Create New Message	Ctrl+N (when in the Inbox)
	Ctrl+Shift+M (from anywhere in Outlook)
Convert HTML Msg to Plain Text	Ctrl+Shift+O (from inside the message)
Flag for follow-up	Ctrl+Shift+G
Forward Message	Ctrl+F
Mark Message as Read	Ctrl+Q or Mark as Unread
Move to Folder	Ctrl+Shift+V (from inside a message)
Reply to Sender	Ctrl+R
Save to Drafts Folder	Ctrl+S
Send Message	Ctrl+Enter or Alt+S
Switch to Inbox	Ctrl+Shift+I
Switch to Outbox	Ctrl+Shift+O
Contact Keyboard Shortcuts	
Create New Contact	Ctrl+N (when in Contacts)
	Ctrl+Shift+C (from anywhere in Outlook)
Create New Distribution List	Ctrl+Shift+L
Open Address Book	Ctrl+Shift+B
Calendar Keyboard Shortcuts	
Accept Meeting Request	Alt+C. To decline a request Alt+D.
Create New Appointment	Ctrl+N (when in Calendar)
	Ctrl+Shift+A (from anywhere in Outlook)
Create New Meeting Request	Ctrl+Shift+Q
Go Forward, Backward one week	Page Down and Page Up
Go to a Date	Ctrl+G
Go to Today's Date	Alt+D
Open an Appointment	Double-click
Task Keyboard Shortcuts	
Create New Task	Ctrl+N (when in Tasks)
Create New Task Request	Ctrl+Shift+U (from anywhere in Outlook)
Open Task	Ctrl+Shift+K
Other Keyboard Shortcuts	
Advanced Find	Ctrl+Shift+F
Check Spelling	F7
Create New Folder	Ctrl+Shift+E
Delete Message, Contact, Calendar Item, or Task	Ctrl+D or Delete Key
	Shift+Delete Key to Bypass Deleted Items folder
Go to Folder	Ctrl+Y

Leave Messages on the Server While You're on the Road

When you check email on the road using Webmail, you may want to leave undeleted messages on the server so you can download them to your regular computer once you're back at the office.

1. Click **Tools, Accounts**.

2. Select the mail account you want to modify, then click **Properties**.

3. Click the **Advanced** *tab*, then tick the check box labeled **Leave a copy of messages on server**.

Log Off at Public Mail Stations

When you access your email from a public station, before you log off, take a moment to clear the memory cache.

From Explorer: Click Tools, Internet Options, Delete Files, Delete all offline content, OK, Clear History, Yes, OK. Now it's safe to log off.

From Netscape: Click Edit, Preferences, Advanced, Cache, Clear Memory Cache and Clear Disk Cache, OK. Now it's safe to log off.

Use Out of Office Email Feature

During an extended absence, you could opt to use the Out of Office Assistant to create and send autoresponse messages back to people sending you messages.

My advice is not to use this feature if you're in an environment that gets a lot of SPAM because you'd be letting SPAMmers know your email address is valid. And not to mention that now they know you're out of the country for two weeks!

1. From the Inbox folder, click **Tools, Out of Office Assistant**.

2. Complete the dialog box.

3. Later, when you open Outlook, you'll be asked if you want to turn off the Out of Office message.

Create a Disposable Email Address

If you leave your address in a chat room, NewsGroup, etc., it will be harvested by SPAMmers 100 percent of the time. One concept that's really cool is the ability to generate a disposable email address you can use that will point email sent to this address to your real address. The disposable email address will self-destruct after a certain period of time that you set. If you shop on the Web, temporary email addresses could be a perfect solution instead of entering your real address.

Below are some Web sites with more information.

www. emailias.com   www. jetable.org
www.SPAMex.com   www.SPAMgourmet.com

☛ *You could also set up regular email accounts in Outlook and create and delete them as needed, but you may have to wait a couple of days for your service provider to activate the new address.*

Create a Distribution List

A distribution list is a collection of contacts that make it easy to send messages to a group of people. It's an alternative to using the Category and filtering feature explained earlier (starting on page 70). When you send a message using a distribution list, recipients will see all the names unless you blind copy (Bcc) everyone (see page 74 for more information on Bcc).

If you're on Microsoft Exchange, your Global Address List can contain distribution lists that will be available to everyone on your network. Otherwise, you can create personal distribution lists.

Create a Distribution List from Names in a Message

1. (Outlook version 2002 or above) From the email message that has the names you want to copy, select the names, click **Edit, Copy** (or right-click the selected names, click **Copy**).

2. Click **File,** point to **New,** click **Distribution List** (or **Ctrl+Shift+L**).

3. In the **Name** box, give your distribution list a name you'll remember, and click **Select Members**.

4. On the right side of the dialog box, in the list, **Add to distribution list**, right-click anywhere inside the box, and click **Paste**.

5. Click **Save and Close**.

Create a Distribution List with Names from Address Book

1. Click **File,** point to **New,** click **Distribution List**.

2. In the **Name** box, give your distribution list a name you'll remember.

3. Click **Select Members**.

4. In the **Show names from the** drop-down list, click the address book containing the desired email addresses (e.g., Contacts).

5. In the **Type Name or Select from List** box, type the name (or first few characters) of the person you want to add to the list. When the name appears in the list below, **double-click** it to move it to the **Add to distribution list** window on the right side.

6. Continue to add desired names, then click **Save and Close**.

Create a Distribution List from Scratch

You may not have the names you want to add to a distribution list already in an email or in your Address Book. You can still create a list (or add people to any of your other distribution lists).

1. Click **File**, point to **New**, click **Distribution List**.

2. In the **Name** box, give your distribution list a name you'll remember, then click the **Add New** button.

3. In the **Add New Member box**, type the person's name and email address. **Repeat Step 4** until you're finished, then click **OK**.

To update information on anyone in a distribution list, open your distribution list, double-click the name, and make desired changes. To delete someone, click their name, then click the **Remove** button (not the Delete toolbar button. If you use the X button, you'll delete your entire list. You'll later find it in your Deleted Items folder).

➥*I've created five different media lists using this method. They all begin with NEWS to keep them together when filed away.*

Send Distribution Lists or Contacts to Another User

There may be times when you want to share a distribution list with another user. You can do this by emailing it.

1. From Contacts, either click **Tools**, **Find**, or click on the Address book icon ▦, or scroll to find the distribution list (or the contact) you want to send. Click it once (or double-click). Then press **Ctrl+F** to send the distribution list or Contact as an email attachment.

2. Complete and send the email message as you normally would.

The recipient will open the message and drag the distribution list icon to his or her Contacts folder (or click **Save and Close**).

From inside a message, you can send a Contact or Distribution list:

1. From inside a new message, click **Insert, Item**, click **Contacts** folder. Then, in the Items window, type the first few characters of the desired name.

2. Double-click the list when it displays to add it to your message as an attachment.

☛*You could use this feature to quickly send your vCard (virtual business card) to someone requesting your contact information. If you haven't added yourself as one of your Contacts, now is a good time.*

Calendar

Use Words in Your Outlook Date and Time Fields

When you set dates in a date field, you can click the drop-down arrow to select a date from the Calendar. But incredibly, you can also type words such as tomorrow, yesterday, 30 days, next Thursday, New Year's Day. Outlook will interpret the word(s) and automatically insert the correct date.

When you type the name of a holiday, this only works if the holiday falls on the same date every year (e.g., Christmas). If you type in the name of a holiday that's already passed, Outlook will put in the date for the current year, not the date for that holiday for the next year.

☛ *Ctrl+G is the shortcut to Go To Date. It also works here.*

View Nonconsecutive Dates on Your Calendar

You can view your calendar a day, week, or month at a glance (click **View** and choose, or click one of the toolbar buttons on the

Standard Toolbar ⑦ inside the Calendar). You can also view nonconsecutive dates on your calendar. This feature could be used when someone sends you several possible meeting dates to choose from.

You'll need to use the **Date Navigator** (the tiny calendar on the right side of the window that depicts a month or two at a glance. If you don't see it, hold your mouse over the very top edge of the TaskPad until it turns into a set of parallel lines with arrows pointing up and down. Now click firmly and drag downward. To view more months in the Navigator, continue to drag downward or to the left, pressing firmly on the mouse.

1. From the Date Navigator, click the day you want to view.

2. Hold down the **Ctrl** key as you click to select up to 14 nonconsecutive days to view.

✎▷ *On your regular Calendar, you can view various numbers of days using **Alt**+ any number between 0 and 9 to see the current day plus a number of next days. For example, Alt+6 will show you today and the next 6 days (0 will show 10 total days).*

Schedule a Meeting With Your Inbox and Empty It

Are You Ready? You should have already organized your paper and computer files, and reworked your Inbox with the step-by-step instructions explained earlier. It's important to do this before you tackle that mountain in your Inbox. If you haven't, go back now. And SPAM should no longer be a problem because you've downloaded SpamNet software. If you haven't, stop now and do it (www.cloudmark.com).

On the other hand, if you've finished organizing everything and added your toolbar buttons, etc., you should schedule a meeting with your Inbox. You're going to be there awhile, and you shouldn't end the meeting until you've finished (or at least put a big dent in it. If you need to stop, schedule another meeting before you go on to something else).

YOUR GOAL:
To always see the
bottom of your Inbox
without scrolling.

Deal with each message in your Inbox and do something with it. Spend two-three hours with this until you finish (however long it takes). Be brutal, and don't let anything stop you. Ignore the pager, the phone, and the knocks on the door. Celebrate when you finish, and let me know about your success!

With each message, here's what you'll do:

- **Make it stop**. If you're getting jokes, newsletters, and any other information you don't have time for or don't want, ask people you know personally to stop. For the rest, fight SPAM through a good ISP who does a great job on the server side, and SpamNet will handle the rest.

- **Delete brutally**. If you haven't looked at the message in months, delete it. If you don't need to keep the information for legal reasons, or it's not something you value, delete it. If you can get the information somewhere else, delete it. And if you can live with the consequences of having trashed something you may need later, delete it. Bear in mind that eighty percent of information you file away will never be referred to again. (Holding down the Shift key when you press Delete removes the item from your computer instead of sending it to the Deleted Items folder.)

- **Do the work if it's quick**. If you can do the work in 2-5 minutes, go ahead and do it. If it'll take longer, schedule it to do later (unless it's hot and absolutely must be done now!).

- **Schedule time to do it later**. Schedule time to work on projects on your calendar the same way you do meetings. Drag the message to your calendar, and set a date to do the work. Then delete the message from your Inbox. Or you can drag the message to your Tasks list and set a reminder date.

- **Note it on your to do list (or drag to Tasks folder), delete the message from the Inbox, and keep going**. Keep all your to do's in one place. I use a spiral notebook. I check off work as I do it, and highlight the work that still needs to be done.

- **File it only if you must**. Store documents either in one of your Inbox folders or a My Documents folder. Don't keep it just because someone sent it to you or just in case. In case what?

- **Pend it and wait.** Pending does not mean something you're procrastinating about. You pend work because you need information that someone else has. Or there is some reason you can't start on the work. Drag the item to your Pending folder (you create this), set a calendar reminder to check the folder once a week, then delete the item from your Inbox.

- **Follow up on it later**. Move a message to your Calendar and set a date to follow up on it (**Ctrl+Shift+V**). If you're using Outlook 2003, flag the message (**Ctrl+Shift+G**), and it'll automatically move into a Follow-Up folder. Don't forget to set a reminder date.

- **Delegate it, then follow up**. If you're fortunate enough to have someone you can delegate work to, send the message as a Task Request email instead of a regular email. This adds the request to your Tasks list automatically.

- **Print it only if you must**. Print emails only if you absolutely have to because it adds to clutter faster than you think.

Create a system and a home for the paper once it's printed (other than a pile on your desk).

Later...

It's time to celebrate! Now, all you have to do is maintain. Remember, you should always do something with every email message you open because your Inbox is for temporary storage only. Always keep your eye on the bottom of the list: you should always be able to see it without scrolling.

Back Up Your Data

Don't lose all your hard work. Schedule a reminder in Outlook to back up important data.

Back Up the Inbox

1. From inside your Inbox, click **File, Import and Export**.

2. Click **Export to a file, Next**.

3. Create a file of type: Personal Folder File (**.pst**), **Next**.

4. Select **Inbox**, and tick to include **subfolders, Next**.

5. Choose where you want to save files by clicking **Browse** (if you don't want the default location), and choose the desired **Option**, click **Finish, OK**.

Back Up Your Contacts

You'll repeat the same steps you did when you backed up your Inbox, except in Step 4, select your **Contacts** folder.

➡️*You can only open a .pst file from within Outlook.*

Back Up Your Rules

1. From the **Inbox**, click **Tools, Rules Wizard**.

2. (In Outlook 2000, go to Step 3.) In the **Apply changes to this folder** list, click the **Inbox** you want.

3. Click **Options**, then click **Export Rules**.

4. In the **Save in** box, decide on where you want the file to be stored, name the file, and click **Save**.

Restore Items in a Data File

Restore Items by Dragging from the .pst Data File

1. Click **File**, point to **Open**, then click **Outlook Data File** (or Personal Folders File .pst).

2. Find the .pst file you want, click it, then click **OK**.

3. Move or copy items in the folder that you opened to the folder you want to restore items to.

4. To close the data file folder, right-click it, and click **Close** *"Folder Name"* on the shortcut menu.

Restore Items by Importing a .pst File

1. Click **File**, click **Import and Export**.

2. Click **Import from another program or file**. Click **Next**.

3. Click **Personal Folder File** (.pst). Click **Next**.

4. In the **File to import** box, specify the path and filename of the .pst file you want to import.

5. Choose one of the following:

    o **Replace duplicates with items imported**. Any existing data in the folder to which you are importing will be overwritten.

    o **Allow duplicate items to be created**. Existing data in the folder to which you are importing will not be overwritten with the information in the .pst file.

o **Do not import duplicate items**. Existing data in the folder to which you are importing will be kept, and any duplicate information in the .pst file will not be copied to the folder.

6. Follow the remaining instructions in the **Import and Export Wizard**. Outlook copies the items from the .pst into the folder you specify.

Eliminate Duplicates in Outlook

It is common to end up with duplicate email messages, contacts, and calendar items. The problem originates when you either perform backups or sync with your PDA. I've researched this, but haven't found out why this happens. The Duplicate Contacts Eliminator at www.sperrysoftware.com could help (they also have eliminators for email and appointments).

Mapping Feature

If you have the full address with zip code of a contact, you can display a map of their location or get driving directions.

1. Open the contact you want to map.

2. If you're connected to the Internet, click the **Display Map of Address** icon .

➡ *I paste driving directions into the notes section of a Contact or Calendar item. All this is synched to my iPAQ (Pocket PC). To make it easy to read the directions at a glance while driving, I increase the font size. To do this, select the directions you pasted in the Notes section of a Contact or Calendar item. Then, right-click anywhere on it, click **Font**, and change the size.*

Surfing the Net from Outlook

In Outlook 2000, you can display an Address bar for surfing the Web. Right-click anywhere on a toolbar, and click **Web**. In Outlook 2002 and 2003, the Address bar should be visible by default.

Once you type the URL of the Web site you want to visit, it'll open in Outlook. If you want to drag information from a Web page to your Inbox to send an email or to your Calendar, you can do it right from within Outlook (or use anagram™ on page 81). To re-display all of Outlook, click the **Back to Previous** toolbar button located on the Address bar.

You can add a shortcut to your favorite Web site to the Outlook Bar.

1. To view the Outlook Bar, click **View**, **Outlook Bar**.

2. To add a Web site to it, with the Web site displayed in Outlook, click **File**, point to **New**, and click **Outlook Bar Shortcut to Web Page**.

3. On the Outlook Bar, click **My Shortcuts** to see the new shortcut.

4. Click the new shortcut and drag it up to **Outlook Shortcuts**.

Scenarios

Here are some ways you can put your new skills to work. Compare the way you are currently managing email to the way you will now as a result of this training.

Challenge
Your boss just sent a request for a report, and it's due in a week. John on your staff has all the information to complete the report. You're going to delegate work to John.

Solution
You're going to delegate this work to John by sending a Task Request email message to him, explaining what you need and assigning a due date. You'll insert the original request from your boss as an Item (Text Only option) so John will have the background. You're sending this as a Task Request instead of a regular email message so the work gets added to your Tasks list automatically.

Challenge
You've received an email from a new customer needing directions to your office.

Solution
You've created a Signature that has directions to your office. You send the reply to the customer and insert the appropriate Signature.

Challenge
A co-worker just sent you an email letting you know that while you're out, he's handling a project for you and not to worry about it.

Solution
That's great news, but you may want to save this message in your CYA folder.

Challenge

You received a message from a customer. She needs you to send her another copy of a proposal you had given her because she can't find her copy (you've been to her office and understand why!) She also wants you to call her next Wednesday morning at 10:00.

Solution

This is not a problem for you. You've organized your computer files and your paper files and can put your hands on anything the instant you need it. You find it and send it quickly.

You then drag the closed email over to your Calendar and set the appointment to call her next Wednesday.

Challenge

You've received an email that requires some work on your part. You want to continue doing your email, but you don't want to forget to do the work.

Solution

Drag the closed message to your calendar, and set a time to work on it. If it's something simple, make a note on your to do list to do it. In either instance, delete the message from your Inbox.

Challenge

A co-worker just sent you a detailed (and complicated) explanation of an assignment that's coming up. You're going to help with it, but you have a lot of questions.

Solution

You send your co-worker a Meeting Request suggesting the two of you meet. Complicated work should be discussed by phone or in person first. And with today's technology, meeting via the Web is the next best thing to being there.

Challenge

You get a lot of messages with several attachments. You're now opening each one to see what it is.

Solution

Make it part of your company's email culture that: all attachments have logical names so the recipient knows what it is; the body of the message explains what each attachment is so the recipient knows without opening if it's something they need; and you only send information to people who really have a need to know.

You have learned how to open all attachments at once in Outlook. You've also learned how to save all attachments at once without opening.

If the attachments are photos, you can also select all of them and drag them into a folder you create on your Desktop, then view them as thumbnails.

Challenge

You're going on vacation for a week. You know when you come back your Inbox will be stuffed. Not only that, but no less than ten people will be standing outside your door waiting to see you.

Solution

When you take vacation, say you're coming back on Tuesday, but come in on Monday, and keep the door closed so you can get caught up. No door? Come in over the weekend to do it, or dial in from home.

Challenge

You receive a lot of emails from friends who have retired. They're coming across jokes, prayers, and all sorts of thoughts for the day that you just have to read.

Solution

Ask them to stop. Period.

IMPROVE YOUR IMAGE

Communicating via email is quick and easy. But one of its shortcomings is that it doesn't give people who don't know you much to go on when judging you or your business.

The Right Email Address

Your email address speaks volumes about who you are and the type of business you run or work for. Which correspondent below will be taken more seriously? Which address suggests the correspondent means business?

pd12@freemail.com – Junk. Delete.

cuteseygirl@freemail.com – You've got to be kidding. Delete.

man12@aol.com – Your business is a hobby. That's too bad. Delete.

peggy@duncanresource.com – A company Website. Worth checking out.

Formatting

Use Good Grammar, Capitalization, and Punctuation

You should treat email as you would any other form of business communication, taking care to convey the right message quickly with the right tone, and using standard rules of grammar and punctuation. You will be judged accordingly.

- **Typeface**. Use a typeface that fits your company. If you're a daycare center, a comedian, or you write jokes for a living, you may choose to use a playful typeface such as Comic

Sans. Otherwise, use a font that's more appropriate for a professional business. The same is true for choosing a typeface for your business card, Web site, brochures, etc.

- **Highlight Important Text**. Use bold formatting to highlight due dates or other important information. If you're using plain text emails with bolding turned off, use the asterisk or something similar to help text stand out. Examples include *best* **or** ((Important)). Please don't overdo symbols and exclamation points (one is sufficient).

- **HTML vs. Plain Text**. Not all email clients can accept messages using the HyperText Markup Language or HTML (computer language used to create documents on the Web) the way Outlook does. To be safe, use plain text format as much as possible. You can change the format of your message from inside a message (click **Format** and choose. If you don't see your Formatting toolbar, right-click anywhere on a toolbar, and click **Formatting**). You can also change Outlook Options to automatically format your messages in either HTML or Plain Text (click **Tools**, **Options**, **Mail Format** *tab*, choose your message format).

- **Capitalization**. It's old news, but since this is a book about email etiquette, I'll say it again. Please do not use ALL CAPS in your email communication. That's equivalent to screaming at a person when you're face to face. Capitalizing a heading or one or two words is acceptable, but not entire paragraphs.

Decorated Emails: Designs, Emoticons, and Smileys

People are busy. Emails are piling in. Your sending emails that are simple, clean, and easy to read will help your recipient go through email quicker.

- **Designs**. Decorations slow people down. Some of them block the text and distract from your message. If you're using email for business, keep it professional, and save the decorations for your next crafts project. If you would not have letterhead printed with ivy growing down the side or flowers all over it, you shouldn't create email messages with this either.

- **Emoticons**. If you received an email message with this in it, **:-O,** would you know it means open-mouthed, surprised? Neither did I, and neither will most people. Emoticons are those facial expressions made by a certain series of keystrokes. Most often they produce an image read with your face turned sideways. If you're emailing your friends, and you know they understand what they mean, then go for it. But in business, it's best to omit them.

  If you receive messages with emoticons, you can find out what they mean at:
  www.computeruser.com/resources/dictionary/emoticons.html.

- **Smileys**. Smileys are cartoon-like icons you download and add to your email messages to convey various moods. Like emoticons, these are not appropriate for business use. They're distracting, and you never know how they will translate on the receiving end. Also, many of these free downloads act as spyware (programming that is put on your computer to secretly gather information about you and relay it to advertisers or other interested parties).

Signature Line

You should create a signature line that goes out with each email. You can have several created and choose which one to send, but it's easier to use one that's generic and have one less thing to worry about.

Use the signature line to explain who you are and how to contact you other than by email. If you're in business, you might want to add a line about what you do and a live link to your Web site. Etiquette says to keep your signature line to no more than five lines, but this is one rule I break. At the very least, include your preferred name, work title, and phone number. (See more information on creating Signatures beginning on page 62.)

Composing

Before the advent of email, you could hide the fact that your writing and spelling skills aren't as strong as you'd like. Just like learning how to type will help you breeze through email quicker, so will improving these skills. Do yourself a favor, and seek proper training if you need it.

- **Write descriptive subject lines**. With so many messages to dig through, increase your chances of getting your message opened by writing better subject lines. The first few words are key because that might be all the recipient sees when your message comes through.

  Just as a headline in a media release, the subject line of your email should tell the whole story. If you write a good subject line, the recipient will fully understand what your message is about before they open it. The next time you send a message, think of your subject line as a headline or billboard when you read. Have you made it clear at a glance what your message is about?

- **Make your subject line match the message**. It's easy to pull up an old message someone sent you months ago and hit Reply to ask them something that's totally unrelated to the old message. Please don't do this. Would you send a letter to someone with the subject line about one thing, and the body of the message about something else? Then don't do this with email. Plus, people are prioritizing their email based on the subject, and they may want to file it to use later. (See page 78 on editing the subject line of messages you receive.)

Keep your messages out of the trash by not using words or symbols SPAMmers are famous for such as free, win, $$$, etc.

- **Create a company-wide classification system**. As a team, your company could develop words that introduce subject lines that make it obvious at a glance what the message is about. It's important that everyone knows what the codes mean. These include codes such as:
    - o **MTG** – Meeting.
    - o **AI** – Action Item.
    - o **IR** – Immediate Response.
    - o **END** – Use at the end of a subject line when it includes everything you had to say.
    - o **NRN** – No response necessary.
- **Identify yourself up-front**. You want your message opened. Let people know who you are, how you know them, where you met, who referred you, etc. If you've met them before, don't assume they'll remember.

- **Keep it brief**. You'll want to make your messages brief, but you want to include enough information for the recipient to make the best decision. Don't make them have to send more messages to get the whole story. This wastes everyone's time and adds to email clutter.

Ask for what you want up-front, using short sentences, short lines of text, and short paragraphs. Shorter sentences (15-20 words) are much easier to read. Break up your paragraphs with the start of each new thought, just as you would in normal writing.

- **Use a salutation that fits**. As in a letter, you should address the recipient according to your relationship. If it's someone you know, it's appropriate to address them by their first name. If it's someone you haven't met, you'll want to use Mr., Ms., etc.

- **End your message politely**. End your message the way you would in a letter, although not necessarily with the same verbiage. I end most messages with the word PEACE. This is part of my automatic signature. "Have a productive day" or "Have a great weekend" also work well.

- **Think first, then write**. If you're upset, angry, or emotional about a topic, wait before you start to write. Don't send a message you could be sorry for later. You may also want to complete the To line after you've written and proofed your message.

- **Limit emails to one topic**. It'll be easier for the recipient to prioritize messages and file them later if you limit messages to one topic.

Sending

When you're sending messages, there are things to consider such as what day or time to send them to increase your open rate. Studies show that Tuesday-Thursday are the best days to send your message. If you're trying to reach a high-ranking executive, most of them check email early in the morning. The following are other factors you should consider when sending messages.

- **Send emails using different accounts based on your needs.** You may have several email accounts: one for different businesses, a personal account for family and friends, another for miscellaneous business inquiries, and so on.

Outlook makes it easy to use different accounts for each email you send.

1. For Outlook 2000, from inside an email message, click

   the **Options** button [icon].

2. In the **Send Using** *drop-down box*, choose the email account you want to use for this particular message. Create and send the message as you normally would.

➥ *If this is something you do a lot, you may want to customize your toolbar and add the Send Using button to it (you learned how to do this on page 53).*

If you're using Outlook 2002 or 2003, click the **Accounts** button next to the Send button inside a new message.

▪ **Send or copy others only on a need to know basis**. Don't Reply All or use CC if everyone has no need to know. You may do this because it's easier, but don't we get enough already without receiving messages we don't need?

▪ **Maintain group privacy by using Bcc**. When you want to blind copy someone on a message, use the Bcc feature. If you're sending a message to a group of people and you need to protect the privacy of your list, send the message to yourself and Bcc everyone else (see page 52).

Another way to protect the privacy of your email addresses is to not give them to a third party (Evite, Plaxo, sites with "Send this email to your friends," etc.). I just don't believe that addresses you willingly hand over to a third party stays with them, especially when the service they're offering is "free." And with a service such as Plaxo, whereas you send your contacts an email asking them to update their information, how many times a day do you think someone is sending this to them? It's not just you. And if you're doing this to a customer, shame on you. Ask them for a vCard instead (see page 93).

- **Minimize attachments**. You should send an attachment only to people you know or to people who are expecting it. The following should be considered as part of your company's email culture.

    o   Refrain from sending a message with more than two or three attachments, unless it's been requested.

    o   Take care in giving the attached file(s) a logical name so the recipient knows at a glance what it is and whom it's from.

    o   Mention the attachment, and put a brief description of it inside the body of the email.

    o   Remember to actually attach the file. As soon as you type the word "attached" or "attachment," stop right then and do it.

    o   Get permission first, especially if it's outside your company and not part of your regular business or over 50k.

- **Don't overuse the high priority option**. If you overuse this feature, few people will take it seriously. A better solution is to use descriptive subject lines and get to your point quickly.

- **Don't overuse the Delivery and Read receipt message options**. It usually annoys your recipient, and it adds to email clutter. And besides, most of your recipients probably have this featured turned off.

What Not to Send

Email is very convenient, but it's not always the best way to communicate. Put yourself in the recipient's place, and use your best judgment for each situation. Here is a sample of what not to send using email.

- **Last-minute cancellations**. People can't get to email as easily as they can voicemail. If you're canceling a meeting at the last minute (for email, this is within 24 hours of the event), you could send an email, but you should use voicemail as a backup. If it's a large group you meet with regularly, you could consider using an inexpensive service at www.callingpost.com. You enter a list of numbers via the Web, and with a couple of instructions using your phone, you can send a message to everyone on the list.

- **Devastating news**. If you have an employee or a friend you need to deliver bad news to, a phone call will be better.

- **Complex topics or explanations**. When the subject requires a lot of explanation that will assuredly generate lots of questions from the recipient, a phone call, face-to-face, or Web meeting is a better solution.

- **Hoaxes**. Before you send a message to all your friends or associates about some terrible thing that could happen to them, or a virus that could wipe out their entire computer system, check it out first. Always visit www.sarc.com to investigate further. Don't become a virus by clogging the Internet with messages that have zero validity.

- **Junk, chain letters, etc**. It's not just you sending your friend a joke he just has to read: it's you and ten other friends. Often, they're too embarrassed to ask you to stop, so I'm asking you. Stop.

Replying

Etiquette says you should respond to messages within 24-48 hours. But in today's world, people want answers fast and that's too long! If you're organized, keeping your Inbox low, and have turbocharged Outlook as explained earlier, you should have no problems staying on top of email. Consider this:

- **Do not reply to SPAMmers.** Don't waste your time responding to SPAMmers. All you're doing is letting them know that yours is a valid email address, which will increase the amount of junk you receive.

- **Use email quoting or bolding**. When you reply to a message, you should have your program set up to include the original message. Another courtesy is to make it obvious which portion of the email you're responding to. You can use email quoting symbols with the plain text format (but don't make your reply confusing by using too much of this).

  >this part of your reply represents a direct quote from the initial email so the recipient you're replying to knows what you're responding to.

  PEGGY: This is where I'd put my response.
  Or respond without adding your name.

- **Have replies go to someone else**. You may send a message to a group but want the replies to go to someone else. From inside the message, click the Options button and enter the desired address.

- **Autoresponders**. An autoresponder is an automated email that goes out when someone sends a message to its address. They can be useless: "Thank you for your email – This is an Autoresponder – I will get back to you shortly. Regards." And they also respond to SPAMmers.

- **Discourage one word replies**. I know I've probably made some people wonder about my manners because I don't respond to every message. That is, if the only thing I have to say is "Thanks, or OK, or Cool, or Groovy." It would make me crazy if I send a message to 200 people, and 50 of them decide to send me a silly one-word message back to say thanks!

To discourage one word messages, here are some simple lines of text I sometimes include:

- o No reply necessary (NRN).
- o Please only respond if …
- o Thanks in advance (so they're not expecting one back from me).

STAY OUT OF TROUBLE

Just think! The moment you hit that Send button, whatever you just typed can be read around the world in a matter of minutes. The best advice I can offer you about staying out of trouble with email is to remember that it is not private.

- o Network administrators can read it.
- o Companies monitor it.
- o Mishaps occur.
- o Hackers hack it.

Company Email Policy

An email policy should be written and distributed to all employees. In addition, employees should be trained on its importance and monitored to determine adherence.

Companies should implement an email etiquette program in order to project a more professional image, increase employee productivity, and reduce liability that could derive from emails being sent that are libelous, defamatory, racist, or otherwise offensive. (Having an email etiquette program with written policies that have been signed by employees won't guarantee you'll be free of any wrongdoing in the courts. However, it will increase your favor by demonstrating you at least tried to prevent it.)

Simple Email Policy

The following sample is a short policy for companies that allow limited personal use of email.

[This document is offered by Email-policy.com. Enter your company name in the [Company] field and adapt and add rules to suit your company's needs. Note that this document is merely for informational purposes and should not be relied upon as a legal document]	**[Company - Date]**

Email Policy

The purpose of this policy is to ensure the proper use of [Company]'s email system. All messages distributed via the company's email system, even personal emails, are [Company]'s property. You must have no expectation of privacy in anything that you create, store, send or receive on the company's email system. Your emails can be monitored without prior notification if [Company] deems this necessary. If there is evidence that you are not adhering to the guidelines set out in this policy, the company reserves the right to take disciplinary action, including termination and/or legal action. If you have any questions or comments about this Email Policy, please contact your supervisor.

It is strictly prohibited to:

Send or forward emails containing libelous, defamatory, offensive, racist or obscene remarks. If you receive an email of this nature, you must promptly notify your supervisor.

Forward a message or copy a message or attachment belonging to another user without acquiring permission from the originator first.

Send unsolicited email messages or chain mail.

Forge or attempt to forge email messages, or disguise or attempt to disguise your identity when sending mail.

Duty of care

Users must take the same care in drafting an email as they would for any other communication. Confidential information should not be sent via email.

Personal usage

Although the company's email system is meant for business use, [Company] allows personal usage if it is reasonable and does not interfere with work.

Disclaimer

All messages will be appended with the following disclaimer: 'This message is intended only for the named recipient. If you are not the intended recipient you are notified that disclosing, copying, distributing or taking any action in reliance on the contents of this information is strictly prohibited.'

Declaration

I have read, and agree to comply with, the guidelines set out in this policy and understand that failure to do so might result in disciplinary or legal action.

Signature _____   Date _____

Printed Name _____

Extensive Email Policy

The following sample policy is extensive, and is for companies that do not allow any personal use of email.

[This document is offered by Email-policy.com. Enter your company **[Company - Date]** *name in the [Company] field and adapt and add rules to suit your company's needs. Note that this document is merely for informational purposes and should not be relied upon as a legal document]*

Email Policy

The purpose of this policy is to ensure the proper use of [Company]'s email system and make users aware of what [Company] deems as acceptable and unacceptable use of its email system. The [Company] reserves the right to amend this policy at its discretion. In case of amendments, users will be informed appropriately.

LEGAL RISKS

Email is a business communication tool and users are obliged to use this tool in a responsible, effective and lawful manner. Although by its nature email seems to be less formal than other written communication, the same laws apply. Therefore, it is important that users are aware of the legal risks of email:

- If you send emails with any libelous, defamatory, offensive, racist or obscene remarks, you and [Company] can be held liable.
- If you forward emails with any libelous, defamatory, offensive, racist or obscene remarks, you and [Company] can be held liable.
- If you unlawfully forward confidential information, you and [Company] can be held liable.
- If you unlawfully forward or copy messages without permission, you and [Company] can be held liable for copyright infringement.
- If you send an attachment that contains a virus, you and [Company] can be held liable.

By following the guidelines in this policy, the email user can minimize the legal risks involved in the use of email. If any user disregards the rules set out in this Email Policy, the user will be fully liable and [Company] will disassociate itself from the user as far as legally possible.

LEGAL REQUIREMENTS

The following rules are required by law and are to be strictly adhered to. It is **prohibited** to:

- **Send or forward emails containing libelous, defamatory, offensive, racist or obscene remarks. If you receive an email of this nature, you must promptly notify your supervisor.**
- Forward a message without acquiring permission from the sender first.
- Send unsolicited email messages.

- Forge or attempt to forge email messages.
- Disguise or attempt to disguise your identity when sending mail.
- Send email messages using another person's email account.
- Copy a message or attachment belonging to another user without permission of the originator.

BEST PRACTICES

[Company] considers email as an important means of communication and recognizes the importance of proper email content and speedy replies in conveying a professional image and delivering good customer service. Users should take the same care in drafting an email as they would for any other communication. Therefore [Company] wishes users to adhere to the following guidelines:

- **Writing emails**:
  - Write well-structured emails and use short, descriptive subjects.
  - [Company]'s email style is informal. This means that sentences can be short and to the point. You can start your email with 'Hi', or 'Dear', and the name of the person. Messages can be ended with 'Best Regards'. The use of Internet abbreviations and characters such as smileys however, is not encouraged.
  - Signatures must include your name, job title and company name. A disclaimer will be added underneath your signature (see Disclaimer)
  - Users must spell check all mails prior to transmission.
  - Do not send unnecessary attachments. Compress attachments larger than 200K before sending them.
  - Do not write emails in capitals.
  - Do not use cc: or bcc: fields unless the cc: or bcc: recipient is aware that you will be copying a mail to him/her and knows what action, if any, to take.
  - If you forward mails, state clearly what action you expect the recipient to take.
  - Only send emails of which the content could be displayed on a public notice board. If they cannot be displayed publicly in their current state, consider rephrasing the email, using other means of communication, or protecting information by using a password (see confidential).
  - Only mark emails as important if they really are important.
- **Replying to emails**:
  - Emails should be answered within at least 8 working hours, but users must endeavor to answer priority emails within 4 hours.
  - Priority emails are emails from existing customers and business partners.
- **Newsgroups**:
  - Users need to request permission from their supervisor before subscribing to a newsletter or news group.

- **Maintenance**:
  - o Delete any email messages that you do not need to have a copy of, and set your email client to automatically empty your 'deleted items' on closing.

PERSONAL USE

It is strictly forbidden to use [Company's] email system for anything other than legitimate business purposes. Therefore, the sending of personal emails, chain letters, junk mail, jokes and executables is prohibited. All messages distributed via the company's email system are [Company]'s property.

CONFIDENTIAL INFORMATION

Never send any confidential information via email. If you are in doubt as to whether to send certain information via email, check this with your supervisor first.

PASSWORDS

All passwords must be made known to the company. The use of passwords to gain access to the computer system or to secure specific files does not provide users with an expectation of privacy in the respective system or document.

ENCRYPTION

Users may not encrypt any emails without obtaining written permission from their supervisor. If approved, the encryption key(s) must be made known to the company.

E-MAIL RETENTION

All emails will be deleted after 60 days. If a user has sufficient reason to keep a copy of an email, the message must be moved to the folder 'For archiving'.

EMAIL ACCOUNTS

All email accounts maintained on our email systems are property of [Company]. Passwords should not be given to other people and should be changed once a month. Email accounts not used for 60 days will be deactivated and possibly deleted.

SYSTEM MONITORING

Users expressly waive any right of privacy in anything they create, store, send or receive on the company's computer system. [Company] can, but is not obliged to, monitor emails without prior notification. If there is evidence that you are not adhering to the guidelines set out in this policy, the [Company] reserves the right to take disciplinary action, including termination and/or legal action.

DISCLAIMER

The following disclaimer will be added to each outgoing email:
'This email and any files transmitted with it are confidential and intended solely for the use of the individual or entity to whom they are addressed. If you have received this email in error please notify the system manager. Please note that any views or opinions presented in this

email are solely those of the author and do not necessarily represent those of the company. Finally, the recipient should check this email and any attachments for the presence of viruses. The company accepts no liability for any damage caused by any virus transmitted by this email.'

QUESTIONS

If you have any questions or comments about this Email Policy, please contact [Name], [Tel], [Email]. If you do not have any questions [Company] presumes that you understand and are aware of the rules and guidelines in this Email Policy and will adhere to them.

DECLARATION

I have read, understand and acknowledge receipt of the Email policy. I will comply with the guidelines set out in this policy and understand that failure to do so might result in disciplinary or legal action.

Signature: _____   Date: _____

Printed Name: _____

RESOURCES

On occasion, you may want to use a disposable email address instead of your real one (see page 93). This is a link to the top ten disposable email address products.

http://email.about.com/cs/dispaddrrevs/tp/disposable.htm

State SPAM Laws

Find out what the SPAM laws are for states that have passed some type of regulatory guidelines. This page takes you to the summary in case you don't want to read the legalese.

www.SPAMlaws.com/state/summary.htm

Email Policy

www.email-policy.com

Products Mentioned in this Book

anagram™ - www.getanagram.com - transforms any contact or appointment information you can select in a document, on a Web page, or in an email message into an Outlook contact or calendar item (page 81).

Duplicate Appointments/Contacts/Email Eliminator – www.sperrysoftware.com has Outlook add-ins that eliminate duplicate email messages, calendar items, and contacts from Outlook (page 102).

Microsoft Office Internet Free/Busy Service - If you use Outlook 2002 or higher, Microsoft has a service that will allow users who are not on an Exchange network take advantage of this feature (page 50). For more information, visit the Microsoft Office Internet Free/Busy Service at http://freebusy.office.Microsoft.com/freebusy/freebusy.dll.

Outlook Attachment Sniffer - www. rsbr.de - Extracts or removes attachments from all or selected Outlook folders (page 82).

Reminder Manager - www.slovaktech.com – This product integrates with Outlook and provides reminders from any folder (see information on reminders beginning on page 89). Not a free download, but they do have a trial version. Also see the Talking Alarm Clock below.

SpamNet - www.cloudmark.com – Will rid you of at least 98 percent of SPAM (page 27).

Talking Alarm Clock - www.cinnamonsoftware.com – Use this when you need a reminder to really stand out because the newer versions of Outlook put all reminders together in a box together. This product does not integrate with Outlook. It is a free download (see information on reminders beginning on page 89).

Index

ABOUT THE AUTHOR

PEGGY DUNCAN is a combination professional organizer, project manager, and computer trainer. That's a powerful set of skills she uses to help busy people like you get things done! She is available to speak at your company or association on land, at sea, and on the Web.

In lieu of television, Peggy Duncan reads 50-lb computer books, then shares their best tips with anyone who will listen. She'd rather spend money on new software than a new dress, and she loves walking into chaos and establishing calm. It all started with growing up with a mother who always knew exactly where everything was.

After college, Peggy went to work for IBM. It was there she realized how well thought-out processes and procedures and the right kind of employee training made work easier. While at IBM, she received awards totaling over $40,000 for the development of more efficient processes through an employee suggestion program.

Peggy specializes in personal productivity. She loves working with professionals and small business owners to help them save as much as two months a year in wasted time, labor, and energy. She travels nationally and also conducts training and consulting on the Web. She is based in Atlanta, GA, with offices in Washington, DC. Contact her at 770-907-8868 or send an email to peggy@duncanresource.com.

OTHER RESOURCES FROM PEGGY DUNCAN

(See Web site for Details and Order Information)

COPE WorkPak CD of Templates to Get You Organized

Online Catalog of Resources to Get You Organized

TIME CATCHERS[SM] Training Series
Seminars – Workshops

Conquer Email Overload with Outlook Tips and Tricks

Get Organized So You Can Think! Follow Up! Follow Through!

Put Time Management to Work

Computer Magic!: Tips and Tricks in Word, Excel, PowerPoint

PowerPoint for Busy People – Beginning to advanced in 4 hours!

International Training Available
At Your Site – Our Site – And On the Web

www.peggyduncan.com
Subscribe to our free Webzine, COPE.

MORE BOOKS BY PEGGY DUNCAN
(See Web site for order details)

Put Time Management to Work

Peggy wrote this book for busy professionals and small business owners. She uses her expertise as a professional organizer, project manager, and computer trainer to get you back on track.

To order, visit www.PeggyDuncan.com.

Just Show Me Which Button to Click! in PowerPoint 2003

Peggy teaches experienced computer users beginning to advanced PowerPoint in four hours. This book is adapted from that class. Written in plain English without all the fat! Lots of pictures too.

To order, visit www.PeggyDuncan.com.

ORDER MORE COPIES OF THIS BOOK

If you want to help others enjoy email again, send them a copy of this book.

Credit Card

Visit our Web site at www.peggyduncan.com to order with a credit card.

Check or Money Order

If you'd rather send a check, photocopy the order form below, complete and mail it with your payment to the address below. Please make check payable and mail to: **PSC Press,** 1010 Pine Tree Trail, Atlanta GA 30349-4979, **TEL 770-991-1316.** Paying by check or money order could deiay shipment an additional 2-3 weeks.

Purchase Orders – Please call first. Only considered for volume orders.

Our Price (USA) Always check our Web site for price updates	**$24.97** **Check Website for volume purchases.** GA Orders addt 7% Sales Tax
S&H	$6 per book – USA. Email us for international rate. Allow up to 2 weeks, USPS and FedEx Ground **USA**.
Volume Orders	Please call the publisher directly at 770-991-1316 for special volume discounts. Or send an inquiry to pscpress@mindspring.com.

QUANTITY _____ ## Conquer Email Overload

Print Name
_____
First   MI   Last

Company
_____

St Address
_____
                                                              Suite

City/ State/ Zip
_____
City   ST   Zip

Email
_____

Phone
_____
Area Code + Number + Extension

Ask about our **Email Overload Training** Peggy conducts on land, at sea, and on the Web.

www.peggyduncan.com

Printed in the United States
34405LVS00007B/79-105

9 780967 472829